The People-Pleaser Transformation for Women

Learn How & Why to Set Healthy Boundaries & Say Yes to Your No

H.L. Nakamura

Paperback: 979-8-9893393-2-7
Hardcover: 979-8-9893393-3-4
Publisher: Inner Light Press

Printed in the United States of America

Table of Contents

Content Warning

Chapters 1,2,5 and 8 include sections on underlying motivations and behavioral patterns of people-pleasing, the differences between selfishness and self-care, the emotional, physical, relational, career and financial toll of people-pleasing, and navigating others' reactions to your new boundaries. Readers who these topics may unsettle should proceed with caution. Alternatively, these sections may be skipped; doing so will not hinder your enjoyment of the book.

Introduction

For a moment, let us imagine Amanda hosting a dinner party for a couple of her close friends. She had spent the entire week meticulously planning the dinner menu, cleaning her house, and even rearranging her schedule to accommodate everyone's schedule. Amanda simply wanted everything to be perfect, hoping to make everyone happy and avoid any potential conflicts.

As the evening progressed, Amanda noticed that her friend, Inge, seemed a bit off. Inge was not her usual cheerful self and was barely touching her food. Amanda's internal alarm bells went off. She immediately shifted her focus from enjoying the party to ensuring Inge was okay. She started asking Inge if she needed anything, offering different dishes, and even suggesting they change the music to something Inge might like.

Despite Amanda's efforts, Inge remained quiet. Amanda felt a growing sense of frustration and resentment. She had gone out of her way to make everything perfect, yet it seemed like her efforts were going unnoticed. She could not understand why Inge did not appreciate all the hard work she had put in.

Later that night, after everyone had left, Amanda sat down with a cup of tea, feeling exhausted and unappreciated. She realized she had neglected her needs and enjoyment in her quest to please everyone. She had spent the entire evening worrying about Inge's mood instead of enjoying the company of her friends.

Reflecting on the evening, Amanda understood that she could not control other people's emotions or always make everyone happy. This realization hit her when she saw that despite all her efforts, Inge's mood had not changed. Amanda realized that her happiness should not depend on others' reactions. She decided to set healthier boundaries and focus on her well-being. Amanda started journaling about her feelings and practicing self-care, slowly learning to say "no" and prioritize her happiness.

As someone who has struggled with being a people-pleaser for most of my life, I know the problems that affect the emotional, psychological, relational, and physical well-being of a people-pleaser. From an emotional perspective, people-pleasers constantly put other people's needs first before their own. It is like being an unofficial CEO of Everyone Else's Happiness, Inc. When people-pleasers do not receive recognition or appreciation for their efforts, they can feel resentment, anger, and frustration toward those they are trying to please (Moore, 2024). When people-pleasers fulfill other people's desires, goals, and needs, they may be unwilling to do so, or they end up doing it out of obligation, which can result in a vicious cycle of being upset at people who may take advantage of their efforts and then regret sacrificing their desires and needs for them and feel sorry for themselves.

Psychologically, people-pleasers may constantly seek approval or praise from others, known as external validation. This tendency can cause the brain to release dopamine, a neurotransmitter responsible for our brain's pleasure and reward system (Cikanavicius, 2017; Hitchcock, 2024). People-pleasers can become addicted to this dopamine rush that makes them feel blissful, thus reinforcing their behavior to seek external validation (Hitchcock, 2024). It is like getting a "like" on social media but in real life. When people-pleasers constantly rely on seeking approval or praise from others to feel better about themselves, it can cultivate a cycle of always seeking external validation to maintain their self-esteem and confidence.

Moreover, when people-pleasers rely heavily on external validation, it can result in problems with making decisions independently. They may struggle with trusting and valuing their intuition, judgment, and abilities. Seeking others' opinions and advice helps them feel comfortable and confident with the decision they want to make or where their intuition is guiding them. Thus, this hinders their ability to fully develop their identity and values (Hadiah, n.d.).

Furthermore, the continuous fear of disappointing others or facing rejection, neglect of personal needs, and self-sacrificing can give rise to the development of chronic anxiety, stress, or depression (*Signs You're a People-Pleaser*, 2023; Vermani, 2023). It is like signing up for a lifetime membership to the Anxiety Club, with free bonus stress or depression! People-pleasers can also lose their identity, making it difficult to know their true desires, goals, aspirations, and interests because of their deep-seated tendency to be accepted by others. When people-pleasers fear being abandoned or disliked, it can cause them to be codependent in relationships and insecure (*Signs You're a People-Pleaser*, 2023).

In relationships, people-pleasers can lose their authenticity by hiding their true feelings, thoughts, opinions, desires, and needs; this can significantly impact genuine connections and cause communication problems. Family, friends, partners, or colleagues might struggle to know the "real" person behind this front. Building deep, meaningful, and long-lasting relationships can be as challenging for people-pleasers as finding a pair of jeans that fit perfectly after 30. Their people-pleasing tendencies hinder them from having trust and genuine emotional intimacy with the people they care about. As a result, their relationships can feel as superficial as a reality TV show or as unfulfilled as a New Year's resolution by February.

Fear of rejection for people-pleasers is like a weak foundation in a house; it causes the structure of their relationships to crumble because others may lose respect for them when they fail to stand up for themselves and be assertive when necessary. People-pleasers often find it difficult to set and maintain healthy boundaries, resulting in them feeling overwhelmed or mistreated. Without clear boundaries, people-pleasers can attract manipulative individuals who will take advantage of their willingness to accommodate, compromise, and self-sacrifice for those around them; this can lead to feelings of shame, guilt, being trapped, and overall unhappiness (Moore, 2024; Porter, 2024).

The physical well-being of people-pleasers can be compromised in numerous ways. The chronic anxiety and stress from always saying "yes" to prioritizing others' needs and desires can lead to the manifestation of physical symptoms, such as headaches, muscle tension, and fatigue (Guttman, 2023). These physical symptoms can be managed with self-care practices, such as regular exercise, a balanced diet, and getting adequate sleep, to name a few self-care tips. However, people-pleasers often neglect it. There are more complex physical problems that chronic stress and anxiety can cause that will require a medical professional to treat, such as insomnia, digestive issues, high blood pressure, a weakened immune system, and unhealthy coping mechanisms that can lead to being addicted to alcohol or other substances (Bastos, 2024; Guttman, 2023). It is like your body is staging a full-on rebellion, and you are the last to know! If you struggle with one or more of these problems, you have the power to manage them, and with this book as your companion, it is even possible to overcome them.

You bought this book because you recognize the toll people-pleasing behaviors have had on your life. I commend you for recognizing you have a problem, which is the first step toward change. Whether it is eliminating the stress and anxiety from prioritizing others' needs or struggling to assert your boundaries, the desire to change is a powerful motivator. Understanding this, I will provide insightful information and draw from my experience to teach you how to navigate boundary setting with self-respect, mindfulness, and emotional integrity. I will guide you in reclaiming respect and autonomy in your relationships by communicating your true feelings, thoughts, needs, desires, and opinions. It is like finally being able to say, "No, I do not want to host the family reunion this year," without feeling guilty. You will gain practical coping mechanisms and advice on establishing and maintaining boundaries effectively, ultimately overcoming your people-pleasing habits.

Addressing people-pleasing habits can significantly impact your overall wellness, relationships, career, finances, and long-term success. Learning to check in with yourself to find out how you are feeling can help you reduce stress and anxiety from constantly trying to please others (*Signs You're a People-Pleaser*, 2023). You can improve your mental and physical health by prioritizing self-care and learning skills such as assertiveness and self-confidence. Setting and maintaining boundaries and communicating your thoughts and needs is crucial to protecting yourself from being overwhelmed, manipulated, or taken for granted (Cohen, 2024). It fosters healthier, mutually respectful, fulfilling, and more balanced relationships and helps you build confidence in expressing your needs and standing up for what you want. People-pleasing in a career context results in burnout and less job satisfaction (Guttman, 2023). Constantly saying "yes" to more tasks can overwhelm you, negatively affecting your work performance. It is like trying to juggle flaming torches while riding a unicycle—impressive but unsustainable. Improving your time management skills, prioritizing your workload, and enhancing your productivity can help you experience greater job or career satisfaction.

Suppose you experience financial challenges due to feeling pressured to assist family members, friends, or partners with money you do not already have in your bank account to gain approval or avoid conflict. In that case, this can lead to poor financial decisions impacting your goals, needs, and desires and accumulating more debt. Setting financial boundaries and learning to say "no" will help you manage your finances better and achieve long-term financial stability. Ultimately, overcoming people-pleasing habits will help you achieve long-term success. It is like realizing you cannot pour from an empty wine glass—working on yourself is the first step toward achieving your goals and aspirations. Addressing your people-pleasing habits will help you no longer seek validation from others, gain greater self-confidence, personal growth and development, get to know yourself better, do things that align with your values, and succeed more in various aspects of life.

Before picking up this book, you probably had the following questions:

- How can I set healthy boundaries and stay firm as someone who has struggled with people-pleasing most of my life?

- How do I establish and maintain psychological, emotional, and relational well-being while navigating my boundary-setting journey?

- How do I achieve self-preservation by setting boundaries in different life contexts?

Reading this book will answer these questions and offers numerous benefits to navigate and overcome people-pleasing habits. The book delves into the psychological and philosophical roots of the underlying behaviors and motivations for people-pleasing. You will gain valuable insight into your behaviors and motivations, learn how to meaningfully say "yes," and craft a new version of yourself that is more firm, empowered, and confident. One of the book's core themes is the importance of self-care and self-compassion practices. Learning strategies to prioritize your needs and well-being is essential to breaking free of the people-pleasing cycle.

You will find practical advice and tips on setting and maintaining healthy boundaries, building self-esteem and self-confidence, communicating effectively, and asserting your needs, which are crucial to fostering healthy and balanced relationships. The book also includes real-life examples, experiences, scenarios, and my personal accounts that illustrate the challenges and successes of overcoming people-pleasing habits. I hope these stories will make you feel like you are not alone and motivate you to implement the practical advice and strategies discussed.

Furthermore, as you read this book, you will be encouraged to reflect on your people-pleasing behaviors and become aware of their impact on your relationships and well-being. You will learn to value your ability to prioritize your schedule, make your own decisions by taking time to think things through and trust your intuition, find balance, cultivate a space for mutual respect, compromise and understand other people's situations and your own, preserve and respect your personal space and timc, practice self-care, stand up for yourself when someone disrespects your boundaries, and validate your emotions, thoughts, needs, and desires.

This book is a comprehensive guide for overcoming people-pleasing habits and building an authentic, self-respecting, and fulfilling life. Think of it as your arsenal for saying "no" without the guilt, setting boundaries like a self-made businesswoman, and finally putting yourself first. You will feel the relief of not always saying "yes" and the freedom that comes with it. Because let us face it, even Wonder Woman needs a day off!

Suppose you have struggled with insecurity and worked on challenging those negative thoughts about yourself. In that case, you can certainly overcome your people-pleasing habits— with a dash of humor and heaps of self-esteem, self-care, self-validation, mindfulness, and emotional integrity. Imagine this version of your future self:

- Asserting your boundaries without fear of rejection or disapproval and valuing yourself without anyone's approval, thus building a strong sense of self-worth.

- Having this newfound confidence that empowers you.

- Having lower stress and anxiety levels, feeling energized, a calm mind, improved sleep, and good mental and physical health, all because of the decision to prioritize self-care and seeking medical assistance where needed.

- A master at setting and maintaining healthy boundaries in your relationships and communicating your true feelings, thoughts, opinions, desires, and needs with others to foster mutual respect and understanding.

- Politely saying "no" to additional tasks and prioritizing your workload in the workplace, and then your boss decides to promote you.

- Setting financial boundaries to manage your finances more effectively and achieving long-term financial stability and independence.

Let us be honest: Who would not want to be the Beyoncé of boundary-setting? Imagine building a legacy of overcoming people-pleasing habits that inspire others to do the same and succeed in their relationships, careers, and beyond!

I am Heather L. Nakamura, the companion guiding you along this transformative journey. I am a published author, Registered Nurse, and self-love advocate dedicated to helping women embrace their true selves and prioritize their well-being. With my background in nursing and extensive experience working with women, I have witnessed firsthand the impact of self-confidence struggles, lack of boundaries, loneliness, and a sense of numbness in other people's lives. Having overcome challenges with self-confidence and authentic love relationships, I bring a unique perspective and deep empathy to my work and writing this book. I am a mother and business owner of a small medical spa in my hometown and work as a bedside nurse at my local county hospital; these roles have helped me value self-care and better understand the power of setting boundaries. Through my writing and coaching, I aim to empower women to break free from societal expectations, guilt, and shame and embrace their self-worth. Outside my professional life, I enjoy outdoor activities such as walking, hiking, skiing, and camping. I am passionate about traveling, spending quality time with my family and friends, and consciously creating a beautiful life.

In the first chapter of this book, you will gain insights into the underlying motivations and behavioral patterns of why people tend to be pleasers. I will dive deeper into the underlying motivations of people-pleasing, often rooted in a fear of rejection, abandonment, and external validation. I will also dive deeper into the behavioral patterns often rooted in codependency and maintaining a perfect image by striving to meet impossibly high standards.

You will also learn about the typical signs and symptoms of people-pleasing from childhood experiences, societal expectations, and cultural influences that can significantly shape people-pleasing behaviors in adulthood.

Chapter One
The Psychology Behind People-Pleasing

"Don't Set Yourself On Fire To Keep Other People Warm" -Anonymous

L et me introduce you to Sarah, a dedicated professional in her mid-thirties who always seemed to have a smile on her face and a willingness to help. From organizing office events to staying late assisting colleagues with their projects, Sarah was the go-to person for support. But beneath her cheerful exterior, Sarah often felt overwhelmed and unappreciated.

Sarah's people-pleasing tendencies began in childhood. Growing up in a family that valued harmony above all else, she learned early on that people-pleasing was the best way to avoid conflict and gain approval. Her parents often praised her for being considerate and putting her siblings' needs first, reinforcing that her worth was tied to making others happy.

As an adult, Sarah carried these habits into her personal and professional life. She found it difficult to say "no" and often prioritized others' needs over her own; this led to chronic stress and anxiety, as she constantly worried about disappointing those around her. Sarah's fear of rejection and desire for

1

approval drove her to suppress her needs and desires, leaving her feeling drained and resentful.

One day, after another late night at the office, Sarah realized she could not continue this way. She sought help and began working with a therapist specializing in people-pleasing behaviors. Through therapy, Sarah learned to understand the underlying motivations behind her actions and developed healthier coping mechanisms.

She began practicing self-care and setting boundaries, learning to communicate her needs assertively. Sarah discovered that saying "no" did not make her a bad person; it was an act of self-respect. Over time, her relationships improved as she became more authentic, self-respecting, and less resentful.

Sarah's journey was not easy, but it was transformative. She reclaimed her sense of self-worth and built a more balanced, fulfilling life by addressing her people-pleasing habits.

Underlying Motivations of People-Pleasing

People-pleasing is a behavior where one prioritizes others' needs and desires at the expense of their own needs and desires, as well as their well-being (McCormack, 2023). Almost everyone at some point in their lives has donned the people-pleaser hat for a specific reason, whether to make friends, keep a friendship or romantic relationship afloat, be perceived a certain way by others, be liked, or avoid the dreaded conflict. The motivations are as endless as the contents of your handbag (which, let us be honest, could double as a survival kit). But here is the kicker: There comes a time when you look back and realize that what started as a simple act of putting someone else first evolved into a habit that can be detrimental to your overall wellness, relationships, career, finances, and long-term success. It is like signing up for a marathon and realizing halfway through that you are running in stilettos. The tendency to people-please can be deeply rooted in numerous psychological factors.

Understanding these motivations and recognizing this repetitive pattern of behavior in your past and present situations, environments, and relationships is the first step toward addressing your people-pleasing habits, setting boundaries, building healthier relationships, and becoming the fabulous, assertive version of yourself you were always meant to be.

Fear of Rejection and Abandonment

People-pleasers often fear rejection and abandonment because they think if they stop accommodating others' needs, everyone will abandon them faster than a cat at bath time. They worry they will be neglected and hated. They may also fear being excluded, criticized, or not accepted by others, much like the only one without a group chat invite. Their fear of rejection can stem from various sources, such as past experiences of rejection, a desire to avoid conflict, or a deep-seated need to be liked and valued by others. It can lead to instances where they avoid situations where they might be judged or rejected, such as avoiding karaoke night after that one disastrous performance. More seriously, for example, if you are a high achiever at work, you may fear being negatively judged or rejected by your superiors and colleagues if you do not meet their expectations.

The fear of abandonment can stem from various experiences and factors, such as childhood trauma, being raised by a caregiver who was emotionally distant or unavailable, traumatic experiences in past relationships, anxious attachment styles, or mental health conditions like borderline personality disorder (Fritscher, 2024; Pietrangelo, 2019; Villines, 2023). Hence, the self-worth of people-pleasers is closely tied to the approval and acceptance of others, much like a plant's need for sunlight—without it, they wilt.

Low Self-Esteem and Self-Worth

People-pleasers with low self-esteem often depend on others' approval to validate their self-worth because it is deeply engrained into their psyche that their value and worth are contingent on others' opinions (Tanasugarn, 2022a). Take Emily, for example. She frequently seeks reassurance from friends and family. She often asks questions such as, "Do you think I hosted a good dinner party?" or "Do you think I dress well?" Emily's self-esteem is so low that she needs constant validation or praise to feel good about herself. The compliments and reassurances Emily receives from friends and family provide a temporary sense of worth, but it never lasts long.

Another instance of seeking validation is through social media. The anticipation for likes and positive comments after posting personal updates or pictures can become a source of self-esteem. However, this can lead to a cycle of dependency on others' opinions to feel worthy. It is akin to the never-ending quest for the perfect skincare routine—just when you think you have found it, you stumble upon an article that points out mistakes you did not even know you were making.

When adults have a history of making themselves seen as perfect and prioritizing others' needs over their own to feel validated and worthy, they can be more susceptible to being manipulated in relationships, especially with abusive or narcissistic people (Tanasugarn, 2022a). Unfortunately, many people-pleasers can end up developing a victim mentality. Instead of being outwardly angry for being manipulated, they get angry at themselves, negatively affecting their self-esteem and self-worth.

The Need for External Validation

External validation is a core motivation for people-pleasing. Philosophers Jean-Paul Sartre, a leading figure in existentialism, and George Herbert Mead, a key figure in symbolic interactionism, have explored how our interactions with others can influence our sense of self and worth. Sartre emphasizes that our daily interactions with others continuously shape our self-perception (*Existentialism Is a Humanism,* 2024; Onof, n.d.). Hence, the concept he developed, known as "le regard" (the look), suggests we become aware of the presence and judgment of ourselves through the eyes of others, leading us to internalize their judgments, thus influencing our sense of worth. So, next time you feel judged for wearing yoga pants to the grocery store, remember, Sartre would say you are simply experiencing "le regard" in action!

Mead's theory, known as the "social self," posits that when we are born, we do not have a predetermined sense of self and worth (Nickerson, 2023). Instead, we gradually develop it through communication and interaction with others as we grow up. Social conditioning plays a role in creating a dependency on external validation. When we learn to see ourselves as others see us, we can rely on others' approval to define our self-worth. It is like when you post a selfie on social media and keep checking for likes—Mead would get it.

B. F. Skinner, one of the philosophers who influenced behavioral psychology, developed a theory known as operant conditioning (McLeod, 2024; *Operant Conditioning*, 2024). It posits that human behavior is influenced and maintained by its consequences. Essentially, we can theorize that habits are formed through reinforcement, which can be either positive or negative. When people-pleasers seek approval, they are looking for positive feedback. The positive feedback they receive results in the positive reinforcement of that behavior, causing them to be more likely to repeat it in the future. This cycle of reinforcement can influence individuals to continue seeking approval to maintain their sense of self. So, if you find yourself baking cookies for the PTA meeting to hear, "These are amazing!" blame it on Skinner and his operant conditioning.

Behavioral Patterns of People-Pleasing

The behavioral patterns of people-pleasing likely stem from one or a combination of a fear of rejection or abandonment, low self-esteem, feelings of unworthiness, or the need to seek external validation, as previously discussed. With this understanding, the people-pleasing cycle can deeply ingrain behaviors that can negatively affect one's growth, development, and well-being over time. It can create a conflict between one's authentic self and the perceived judgments and expectations of others. Additionally, it can be challenging to unlearn patterns of people-pleasing behavior, but it is essential to break the cycle. The behavioral patterns of people-pleasing often manifest through codependency and perfectionism in relationships.

Understanding these behavioral patterns and recognizing how people-pleasing behaviors affect your interactions, well-being, and sense of achievement is crucial. This awareness can empower you to make changes such as setting boundaries, prioritizing self-care, and recognizing intrinsic worth. Embrace imperfection, practice self-compassion, and remember: Your intrinsic worth is not solely tied to achievement. After all, even Catwoman needs a day off to binge-watch her favorite shows and eat ice cream straight from the tub!

Codependency and Relationship Patterns

People-pleasers find themselves in codependent relationships because of several deep-seated psychological factors and learned behaviors. They can go to great lengths to avoid conflict and rejection and to feel worthy and valued by consistently putting others' needs above their own. They often believe they are "nice" for excessively accommodating everyone. It is like they have a PhD in people-pleasing, earned from the University of Childhood Experiences, where they learned that doing what everyone needs and wants is a way to gain approval and avoid negative outcomes. If they grew up in a household where their needs were dismissed or harshly criticized, they might have picked up that prioritizing others' needs ensures security and acceptance (Ball, n.d.).

7

When it persists into adulthood, it can become highly toxic. Individuals can give to others without expecting much in return; they can worry about the pain and abuse they are experiencing in their relationships; and they can feel sorry for themselves and even be confused by the problems happening in their relationships but do not know what to do about them. They might even try to convince themselves that the problems they are experiencing could be worse but are not. People-pleasers in codependent relationships can excessively meet others' needs to maintain harmony and avoid disapproval. Meanwhile, the other person in the codependent relationship can become dependent on the people-pleaser for their needs, perpetuating the cycle.

Excessive self-sacrifice can take a heavy toll on people-pleasers, leading to emotional exhaustion, resentment, and a loss of touch with their needs, desires, and identity. It can also result in increased anxiety and stress and unhealthy relationship dynamics where the needs of the people-pleaser are consistently overlooked (Ball, n.d.; Plattor, n.d.). It is like being the star of a one-person show where the only audience member is never satisfied!

Perfectionism and People-Pleasing

Perfectionists may engage in people-pleasing to maintain an image of flawlessness, like trying to keep a shirt spotless while eating spaghetti. They can strive to meet impossibly high standards due to several psychological and social factors. When people-pleasers define their self-worth by their achievements and productivity, it can lead them to set unrealistic goals to validate their value, gain approval, and avoid rejection—think of it as trying to win a gold medal in the "Olympics of Overachieving."

The need for perfection and external validation can be a coping mechanism for sensitivity to criticism, fear of failure, and an obsession with holding themselves to inflexible, unrealistically high standards. This behavior is often driven by underlying feelings of self-doubt, inadequacy, and guilt and shame when they do not meet those standards (Hopper, 2018; *Perfectionism*, 2024; Swider et al., 2018).

Remember that these underlying motivations and behavioral patterns of people-pleasing can overlap, and your experiences can differ.

The Typical Signs and Symptoms of People-Pleasing From Childhood Experiences, Societal Expectations, and Cultural Influences

Parental influence and conditioned responses from childhood experiences can significantly shape people-pleasing behaviors in adulthood, especially when raised by parents or a caregiver with a particular personality disorder. For example, parents with borderline personality disorder (BPD) have difficulty regulating their emotions and may exhibit behaviors such as guilt-tripping, manipulation, and emotional instability (Lo, 2021; Tanasugarn, 2022b). These parents can one moment shower their children with love and, the next, blame them for things they did not do at all. Children raised by parents with BPD live in a constant state of walking on eggshells as a way to avoid triggering their parent's emotional outbursts. It is like living in a house where the floor is made of bubble wrap—one wrong step and *pop*, an explosion of emotions!

These children often internalize the blame and guilt they are made to feel, which results in feelings of worthlessness and shame (Lo, 2021). When they grow up, they learn to prioritize others' needs before their own, which makes them constantly seek validation and approval to avoid conflict.

Imagine living with a parent who treats affection like a rare Swiss Army knife—only to be seen on special occasions. Parents with Narcissistic Personality Disorder often exhibit behaviors such as a black belt in emotional withdrawal, manipulation, and a lack of empathy (di Giacomo et al., 2023; Lamla, 2020; Telloian, 2021). These parents might pull back emotionally as a means to control and manipulate their children, and interacting with them can be challenging. These children learn to constantly seek approval and validation. It is like trying to get a hug from a cactus—painful and rarely rewarding.

When these children grow up, they feel like they have to earn love and approval, which leads to them unconsciously committing to a lifetime of people-pleasing and low self-esteem. They often develop a hidden talent for reading others' emotions and needs and subsequently put themselves last constantly to avoid conflict and gain affection.

Socialization and cultural relativism play a major role in shaping people-pleasing behaviors. In collectivist cultures, the mantra is often "harmony above all," which leads to a heightened ability to read the room but might cause struggles with asserting personal needs as adults. Conversely, in individualistic cultures, the script might read, "Stand out, be bold, and whatever you do, do not let anyone tell you what to do!" This assertive attitude can create adults who are great at advocating for themselves but might sometimes forget that other people's opinions exist. For example, in many Asian cultures, children are taught to prioritize family and community harmony over their desires, which can lead to developing people-pleasing tendencies as adults (Moore, 2024). This cultural relativism means that what is considered a virtue in one culture might be perceived as a weakness in another.

Cultural influences, such as ethnicity and community values, can significantly shape people-pleasing behaviors in adulthood. Different cultures have varying expectations regarding social behavior, which can impact social interactions. For example, in some African cultures, communal living and interdependence are highly valued, which can foster people-pleasing behaviors as individuals strive to maintain group cohesion (Martin, 2021b). It is like being part of a big family where everyone knows your business, and Auntie Halle's opinion on your life is practically law. Additionally, societal pressures to conform to gender roles can exacerbate people-pleasing tendencies, particularly among women who are often expected to be nurturing and accommodating.

Interactive Element

Take a moment to consider your people-pleasing behavior. Grab a pen and notebook and find a quiet space to reflect without distractions. Write down specific thoughts, feelings, and situations where you have exhibited people-pleasing tendencies. Be honest with yourself and think deeply about the underlying motivations behind these tendencies.

Instructions

1. Identify situations.

Write down specific instances where you found yourself trying to please others at the expense of your needs or desires. For example:

- "I agreed to work overtime even though I was exhausted."
- "I went to a social event I did not want to attend just to avoid disappointing a friend."
- "I agreed to help a colleague with their project even though I had my own deadlines."

2. Explore feelings.

Note the emotions you felt in those situations. Were you anxious, guilty, or resentful? For example:

- "I felt anxious about saying no."
- "I felt guilty for prioritizing my own needs."

- "I felt stressed and overwhelmed."

Understand motivations.

Reflect on why you felt compelled to please others. Was it fear of rejection, a desire for approval, or something else? For example:

- "I feared my boss would think less of me if I did not stay late."
- "I wanted my friend to think I was supportive."
- "I wanted to be seen as a team player and feared they would think I was unhelpful."

By writing these down, you can start to see patterns in your behavior and understand the motivations behind your people-pleasing tendencies. This self-awareness is the first step toward working on healthier behaviors and practicing self-validation.

In the next chapter, you will learn how constantly saying "yes" to other people's demands can lead to stress. I will explore how the fear of disappointing others can create anxiety, especially when thinking about the consequences of asserting your own needs, and how neglecting your needs can lead to resenting those you are trying to please. You will also learn the signs and leading triggers for burnout in people-pleasers and how this can lead to several physical health problems. There is a paradox of people-pleasing in relationships, which I will help you understand. It is essential to value your interpersonal relationships and prioritize others, but finding a balance and practicing self-care is equally crucial. I will also discuss the career implications of overcommitting to tasks and others taking your efforts for granted. Additionally, there are financial implications to providing financial assistance to others to gain approval or avoid conflict, which can impact your financial stability.

Chapter Two
The Cost of Always Saying Yes

"People will love you, people will hate you,
and none of it will have anything to do with
you" -Abraham Hicks

When you constantly say "yes," the cost of your agreeableness is not just measured in time and favors—it is like running a marathon in flip-flops. It takes a silent toll on your physical, emotional, and mental well-being and your relationships, career, and finances. Are you ready to explore the consequences of people-pleasing both personally and professionally? Buckle up because it is about to be a wild rollercoaster ride!

ॐ

Emotional Toll: Stress, Anxiety, and Resentment

Everyone has responsibilities, and constantly saying "yes" to other people's demands can lead to anxiety, avoidance behaviors, people-pleasing, stress, and burnout. The fear of disappointing others is deeply rooted in societal norms and expectations (Franzoni, 2023). In many societies, worth is tied to achievements. This societal pressure to meet expectations can be overwhelming, and it is important to recognize that you are not alone in feeling this way. As a result, when you inherently want to meet social expectations to feel worthy and accepted, the fear of disappointing others will intensify, especially in situations where acceptance and love appear conditional on socially acceptable behavior or achievements. It is like trying to keep up with the latest fashion trends—when you think you have nailed it, skinny jeans are out, and mom jeans are back in!

This fear can create anxiety, particularly when thinking about the consequences of asserting your needs. Our minds can start to imagine negative outcomes such as rejection, criticism, failure, or conflict, which can drive maladaptive coping mechanisms. To escape the risk of failure and the anxiety of potential disappointment, you might avoid situations, opportunities, or challenges where you need to assert your needs, limiting your personal growth. You might engage in people-pleasing behaviors, such as perfectionism, to make others happy out of fear of letting someone down or to overcompensate for this fear. In turn, this can damage your relationships, cause low self-worth, and make you neglect your well-being (Barreca, 2020). It is like trying to balance a career, family, and social life—eventually, something will fall through the cracks.

Conversely, the fear of disappointing others can lead to chronic stress and burnout through unhealthy behaviors or toxic patterns, such as overcommitting and taking on too much or habitually downplaying your achievements (Franzoni, 2023). Think of it as trying to be the perfect mom, partner, and professional all at once—eventually, you will need a break.

Neglecting your needs while trying to please others can lead to resenting those you are trying to please. When your needs go unmet because you constantly prioritize others' needs over your own, it can stir up a cocktail of negative emotions and beliefs. Think of it as a recipe for disaster: A dash of deprivation, a sprinkle of frustration, and a heaping spoonful of overwhelm. These ingredients can fuel your insecurities, low self-esteem, sensitivities, fears, codependency, and conditioned responses, all because you are not taking care of yourself.

Finding yourself always giving and never on the receiving end in your relationships can create a sense of inequity and imbalance. You might start feeling like you are the only one invested in the relationship while the other person is just tossing you breadcrumbs. Over time, this can cause you to harbor feelings of resentment in your heart.

Constantly suppressing your genuine emotions, needs, and desires to avoid conflict or disappointing others can be physically and emotionally draining. It is like running a marathon with no finish line in sight. Feeling physically and emotionally drained can exacerbate resentment, especially when your efforts are not reciprocated or acknowledged.

Physical Consequences: Burnout and Exhaustion

The constant effort to meet others' needs can lead to burnout and exhaustion. Burnout is a form of exhaustion that affects one's physical, emotional, and mental well-being caused by continuous stress, often resulting from working too hard or overextending yourself (*Burnout,* n.d.). It is like your body's way of saying, "I have had enough!"

Burnout can sneak up on you, especially when you are someone who wears many hats. There are common signs of burnout that you can watch out for; let us talk about the physical symptoms first. These can range from chronic fatigue, making it difficult to perform daily activities, even after a good night's sleep (Mayo Clinic Staff, 2023). It is like your bed has a magnetic force you cannot escape. You may have sleep problems, gastrointestinal symptoms (i.e., stomach aches or digestive problems like irritable bowel syndrome), and experience frequent or recurring headaches. Your brain's way of saying, "Can we not adult today?" Other physical health problems are heartburn; increased risk for substance abuse, overeating, heart disease, and hypertension; muscle pain, particularly in the neck, shoulders, and back; and a weakened immune system that increases susceptibility to infections and illnesses (*Burnout,* n.d.; Precker, 2022; Salvagioni et al., 2017; Scott, 2024).

The emotional and mental symptoms of burnout can make anyone feel like a Debby Downer, and these are the telltale signs of them:

- Experiencing concentration problems that make it difficult to focus on tasks or make decisions. It is like your brain's playing hide and seek with your thoughts; even the simplest tasks seem daunting.

- Having a depressed mood that causes you to feel down and hopeless or experience a loss of interest in activities you used to enjoy. Even your favorite TV show cannot cheer you up.

- Feeling a sense of inadequacy or low self-esteem and negative self-talk. Your inner critic is working overtime and is not even getting paid.

- Noticing persistent feelings of cynicism toward your work or life as though you have become the unofficial spokesperson for "meh."

- Experiencing changes in mood, including irritability or anger, may be noticed by those who know you well and recognize these feelings as uncharacteristic (Burnout, n.d.; Scott, 2024).

On the other hand, the behavioral symptoms of burnout can turn you into a hermit, withdrawing from social interactions or activities. It is like putting your social life on a permanent vacation. Also, if you work too hard, a noticeable drop in your work performance, motivation, job satisfaction, or productivity can be caused by burnout (Nortje, 2021). You might even develop a new motto: "Why do today what you can put off until tomorrow?"

The leading trigger for burnout in people-pleasers is feeling like a puppet on a string. Just kidding, but when you are not in control of your tasks or responsibilities at work or home, or even being asked to do something that conflicts with your authentic self, it can lead to feelings of cynicism, fatigue, and a depressed mood (*Burnout,* n.d.). Other triggers include overcommitment, lack of boundaries, and the need for external validation. Even when you do not have the emotional, physical, or mental capacity to take on more responsibility, you might have a knee-jerk reaction to say "yes," which can be exhausting and lead to chronic stress (Chain, 2024; Smith, 2023). It is like trying to juggle flaming torches while riding a unicycle—impressive but not sustainable for long. The fear of conflict can lead to avoiding confrontation, agreeing to things you would not ordinarily do, or deciding not to express your true feelings, creating internal tension while maintaining a facade of harmony in your relationships.

୫

Relationships: The Paradox of Pleasing Others but Losing Yourself

It is not a crime to value interpersonal relationships and prioritize others. However, it is crucial to find a balance, as self-care is necessary for maintaining relationships and living a fulfilled life. The paradox of pleasing others but losing yourself is a complex phenomenon. Suppose you knew or someone told you that making others happy would result in negative consequences for you and your relationships, even though unintentional. In that case, I doubt you would engage in people-pleasing behaviors for the most part.

The paradox of people-pleasing is a misunderstood phenomenon, too. People-pleasers seek validation, approval, and reassurance from others but lose their self-identity and self-worth as it becomes contingent on others' opinions (Vigliotti, 2023). It is like trying to win a popularity contest where the only prize is chronic exhaustion. For example, consider two friends planning a trip together. The friend who is a people-pleaser agrees to stay in more expensive hotels to avoid disappointing the other friend despite being unable to afford it. Unfortunately, this decision leads to increased credit card debt and financial stress for the people-pleaser, while the friend remains unaware of the sacrifice made by the people-pleaser.

People-pleasers can go to great lengths to avoid conflict in their relationships, but this avoidance can create a cycle of miscommunication and unfulfilled needs in their valued relationships (Cohen, 2024). Imagine being so conflict-averse that you would instead agree to watch a 10-hour documentary on the history of paint drying than say, "I would prefer a comedy." For example, Jennifer always conforms to her partner's desires to avoid disagreements that could lead to a potential breakup. Over time, this behavior makes her feel unheard and unappreciated, leading to anxiety and a loss of sense of self. Jennifer's behavior of seeking approval by prioritizing others stems from her childhood experiences and persists in affecting her adult relationships. Authentic communication, the expression of personal needs, and the other person in the relationship fulfilling their responsibilities are crucial for healthy, balanced relationships.

By consistently prioritizing others, people-pleasers can create an imbalance in their relationships. While initially unintended, this can lead to resentment and frustration, both for themselves and for those they are trying to please. When the love, energy, and time you put into the relationship is unreciprocated and unsupported by the other person, it can damage the relationship over time. It is like being the only one paddling in a two-person kayak—eventually, you are simply going in circles. For example, you might take on extra tasks and responsibilities in the workplace to be seen as a team player. Even though your superiors or team show their appreciation for it, overextending yourself can lead to burnout and reduced productivity over time. While unintended, the lack of boundaries and self-care harms you and your team.

Career Implications: Overcommitment and Underappreciation

In a career context, people-pleasing can significantly impact your well-being. From a philosophical standpoint, the choices that people-pleasers make often require moral guidance to shift the value system that supports people-pleasing behaviors. As a human being, you are important, and your welfare is equally important. Sometimes, we do not consider the effects our choices have on our well-being. People-pleasers often struggle with internalizing problems such as fear of rejection or abandonment, conflict avoidance, anxiety, depression, a need for external validation, and low self-esteem. As previously discussed, these issues lead them to prioritize others' needs and desires over their own (Shapiro, 2021).

As a result, taking on more tasks or responsibilities than one can comfortably manage can cause more inconvenience or harm to the people-pleaser than benefit to the team or superiors. Overcommitment often results in a "siege mentality," where you feel overwhelmed by extra tasks and struggle to get the support you need from your team or superiors, feeling like you are constantly under siege by these responsibilities (Tulgan, 2020). It is like being the lone warrior in a never-ending battle, except your armor is made of sticky notes, and your sword is a highlighter.

The worst-case scenario is when you start to not see eye to eye with your colleagues. You know you still need to rely on them, but you resist asking for what you need out of fear of disappointing them and thus becoming increasingly overwhelmed. You make sacrifices, such as spending less time with family, friends, and even yourself, to accommodate the increased workload. While you make more time to accept the increased workload, appreciate the praise for your hard work and commitment, and forgive yourself for accepting unrealistic deadlines, all of this leads to stress and burnout. It is like trying to herd cats while balancing on a tightrope—entertaining to watch but bound to end in chaos.

There are instances where your hard work can go unnoticed. In the workplace, when colleagues or superiors know you will always say "yes" to every request, your constant willingness to help can be taken for granted. Internalizing this underappreciation can make you unfair to yourself. You might avoid conflict and maintain harmony by putting on a smile and carrying on with your work instead of advocating for yourself and your contributions. This lack of self-advocacy can lead to feelings of underappreciation and resentment. Remember, the only person responsible for your success in your career is *you*. It is okay to put your own needs and desires above others, when you want to move forward in your career. Self-advocacy is not just about standing up for yourself but about paving the way for your career advancement. After all, even the powerful women you look up to know when to rest and come back stronger.

Financial Impact: The Price of Saying "Yes"

When you prioritize providing financial assistance to others, it can impact your financial stability, and you may miss out on opportunities to invest in your financial future. Those missed opportunities can result from giving money to others that you do not have to give. It feels good to lend a helping hand to whoever is asking for money in the short term, but it will damage your financial prospects in the long run.

When you keep playing the role of the generous benefactor, your emergency fund (i.e., a safety net of savings that you use to pay for unexpected expenses in the future) might start looking like a desert—dry and barren. Remember, even hard-working people like yourself must put money away for retirement or invest in opportunities for wealth creation over time.

Emotional decision-making can lead to poor financial decisions. That rush of satisfaction from supporting someone close to you who is in financial need is like a sugar high—it feels great at first, but it wears off quickly and leaves you with financial stress and anxiety. Especially if it strains your budget, you might find yourself in a situation where your wallet is crying louder than a toddler who dropped their ice cream. Also, if you already have debt, constantly providing financial support can put you in a bad financial position by increasing your debt faster than you can say "credit card bill."

In hindsight, your financial needs come first, and everything else follows. There is a golden financial principle that I stand by that says, "Pay yourself first." If I am honest, I do not always get it right. Sometimes, I fall into the trap of prioritizing others' financial needs before my own and say, "I will pay myself back the money I did not pay myself first with this salary or with this sum of money I have received to help my family." Spoiler alert: It rarely works out as planned.

I usually record the money I should have paid myself first and do so as soon as possible. Money given to others can derail financial goals you could have achieved or make them unattainable if your money is constantly diverted to assist others. It is like trying to fill a bathtub with the drain open—no matter how much you pour in, it never fills up.

Interactive Element

Take a moment to create an imaginary balance sheet to assess the costs and benefits of your people-pleasing tendencies. This exercise will help you see how your choices impact various aspects of your life and encourage reflection on setting healthier boundaries.

Instructions

1. **Draw a balance sheet**: Divide a page into two columns. Label the left column "Costs" and the right column "Benefits."

2. **Identify aspects of life**: Consider different aspects of your life such as physical health, emotional well-being, career, relationships, and finances.

3. **Assign values:** For each aspect, write down the costs and benefits of your people-pleasing behavior. Be honest and specific.

Example

	Costs	Benefits
Physical health	Feeling exhausted from overcommitting Lack of time for exercise	Occasional appreciation from others
Emotional well-being	Increased stress and anxiety Resentment towards others	Temporary sense of approval
Career	Overworking and burnout Neglecting personal projects	Positive feedback from colleagues
Relationships	Feeling taken advantage of Difficulty setting boundaries	Being seen as reliable
Finances	Spending money to please others	Avoiding conflict

Reflection

- **Physical health**: "I often feel exhausted because I overcommit to helping others, leaving little time for exercise."

- **Emotional well-being**: "I experience increased stress and anxiety, and sometimes feel resentment towards those I try to please."

- **Career**: "While I receive positive feedback from colleagues, I often overwork and neglect my projects."

- **Relationships**: "I feel taken advantage of and struggle to set boundaries, even though I am seen as reliable."

- **Finances**: "I spend money to please others, which impacts my financial stability."

By completing this balance sheet, you can visualize the impact of your people-pleasing tendencies on your life. This awareness can help you make more balanced choices and set healthier boundaries.

In the next chapter, you will learn how to make intentional choices that benefit your well-being. You will also learn to identify your true desires and needs in situations, relationships, and daily interactions. No more saying "yes" to that third cousin's cat-sitting request unless you want to.

I will discuss how you can align meaningful "yes" moments with your values. Imagine only agreeing to things that make your heart sing rather than your stress levels spike. I will explore how to trust yourself and listen to your instincts, which hold so much wisdom.

You probably have heard of a mission statement. But have you heard of a personal mission statement? I will explore its two elements to encourage you to envision the person you want to be and what you want to accomplish with your life. There are benefits to creating a personal mission statement, which you can use to overcome your people-pleasing habits.

Chapter Three
The "Yes" That Matters

"The only people who get upset when you set boundaries are those who benefited from you having none." -Unknown

---

D id you ever think a meaningful "yes" would lead to taking care of yourself? If yes, you will surely enjoy making intentional choices, achieving your goals, and aligning your actions to your values to enhance self-care.

Learning to Say "Yes" to Yourself

You can make intentional choices that will ultimately benefit your well-being. Even as a people-pleaser, you can start learning to identify your needs and wants to break the people-pleasing cycle and prioritize your needs. Understanding what truly matters to you and what you want is the first step in making intentional choices. Take the time to reflect on your needs and desires in life. You can ask yourself questions such as "What truly makes me happy?" "What are my core values and beliefs?" "What are my short-term and long-term goals?" After identifying your needs and desires, you can practice asserting them. Remember, it is okay to put yourself first sometimes. Think of it as putting on your oxygen mask before helping others.

I will discuss practicing assertiveness in more detail later in the book. However, I will touch on assertiveness briefly for now. Assertiveness is vital for setting boundaries and building healthy relationships by confidently expressing your needs, desires, and thoughts and ensuring they are clearly understood while respecting others. People-pleasers often struggle with being assertive out of fear that being honest and direct will result in conflict or hurt the other's feelings.

Saying "no" to others is saying "yes" to yourself. Practice assertiveness by using clear and direct "I" statements. For example, "I feel stressed when I accept unrealistic deadlines, and I need help with moving some deadlines around." It is also essential to learn how to use a firm but respectful tone of voice when saying "no." You might find this challenging, but it is crucial for setting boundaries and managing stress. Remember, "No" is a complete sentence. Use it wisely, like a secret superpower!

Setting healthy boundaries is essential to learning to say "yes" to yourself. Boundaries help you protect your mental and emotional health, time, and energy, allowing you to focus on what matters to you and to decline requests that do not serve your well-being. It can also be challenging at first to set boundaries, but with practice, it will become second nature. After establishing your boundaries with others, take some time to revisit and adjust them as needed to ensure they are still working in your favor. Think of boundaries as your personal force field—keeping the drama out and the peace in.

Learning to say "yes" to yourself involves prioritizing self-care. I will discuss self-care in a later chapter of the book. Self-care means making time for activities that rejuvenate and energize your physical, emotional, and mental health, whether it is exercise, hobbies you enjoy, getting enough sleep, seeking support from family, friends, or a mental health professional, or simply relaxing on the couch with your favorite cup of tea or coffee. So, schedule that personal time with yourself—doctor's orders!

People-pleasers often want to be seen as perfect across all life domains. When they are seen as imperfect, it can lead to feelings of inadequacy and failure. But here is the thing: Perfection is overrated! Accepting imperfection and embracing mistakes for what they are is good; these are lessons that are part of your evolution. Think of them as life's quirky little plot twists. This mindset can significantly reduce self-perceptions of not being enough and feeling like a failure while increasing self-compassion.

It is common for people-pleasers to struggle with negative thoughts about themselves, such as "I cannot handle conflict" or "I am responsible for others' happiness." These thoughts can make people-pleasers do everything they can to make others happy and avoid conflict. Overcoming these negative thoughts is vital to learning to say "yes" to yourself. One way you can overcome negative thoughts is to assess whether they are true by asking questions such as "Are these negative thoughts based on factual information or assumptions? Can I think of more positive and accurate interpretations? Another way to overcome negative thoughts is to reframe them into positive thoughts. For example, rather than saying, "I cannot handle conflict," you can say, "I can confidently express my thoughts and actively listen to what the other person has to say." It is a great way to practice self-compassion, too.

You do not have to break the people-pleasing cycle alone. It is crucial to have a robust support system that includes friends, family, and, importantly, a mental health professional to seek guidance and encouragement from and to hold you accountable. Therapy, in particular, is a powerful tool for understanding the underlying behaviors and motivations of people-pleasing and developing new coping mechanisms. It provides a safe space for exploration and learning. Surrounding yourself with supportive individuals can also make a significant difference in your journey. Think of them as your personal cheer squad, pom-poms optional.

Identifying Your True Wants and Needs

Your relationship with yourself is fundamental to identifying and responding to your needs and wants. It is integral to building a fulfilling life (Tartakovsky, 2015). Self-reflection and questioning can help you regularly practice self-compassion and self-care.

Self-reflection is an excellent tool for understanding what is truly important to you and what would fully satisfy you. Take time to assess what truly matters to you and what brings you joy and satisfaction in various areas of your life, such as your career, relationships, daily interactions, dreams and passions, personal growth, or even emotional, physical, and mental well-being.

By regularly reflecting on different areas of your life, you can clearly understand what you need and desire to unlock a fulfilling and content life. This process will help you identify what aspects of these areas do not align with your values, needs, desires, and the broader context of your life. Then, consider what truly matters and what would be ideal in each area of your life without any restrictions or fear. Be honest and specific, and write these down in great detail.

Asking yourself questions can be powerful. Imagine you have been attending therapy sessions with a specialist on people-pleasing behaviors. At the end of the last session, you look back and say, "This has been the best decision and use of my time, energy, and money." What needs to happen for you to say this about every area of your life? Another thought-provoking question based on this would be: "If you were having this conversation with someone two years from now, and you were looking back over those two years, what must have occurred in your life for you to feel joyful and satisfied with your growth?

Questions help us go through a journey of self-discovery about our needs, dreams, passions, and desires. They also assist with our decision-making, understanding ourselves better, and ensuring we keep progressing in life.

Here are questions that can help you identify your needs and desires:

1. How do I feel about how I have been taking care of myself?

2. What activities make me feel most fulfilled and happy?

3. Where do I feel content (in the different areas I have chosen above)?

4. What would I spend my days doing if money and time had no constraints?

5. What activities, limiting beliefs, and behaviors am I consciously or subconsciously saying "yes" to that I want to release?

6. What are the things I often daydream about or find myself wishing for all the time?

7. What activities, positive beliefs, and behaviors am I consciously or subconsciously saying "no" to that I would like to embrace?

8. What goals or achievements would make me feel proud and accomplished?

9. What boundaries do I need to establish to help protect my time, energy, money, and myself?

10. What aspects of my life now do I wish were different, and how would I change them?

Please remember, you do not need to do anything to ask yourself what you need. Also, you do not need anyone's permission to respond to your needs. Finally, use your time and resources to focus on your dreams and passions and speak up for yourself. You also do not need to do anything to deserve to engage in relaxing, joyful activities. After all, even Wonder Woman swaps her lasso for a latte sometimes—because even superheroes need a break to recharge.

All you have to do is stay true to yourself.

Aligning Your Actions With Your Values

Aligning meaningful moments of saying "yes" with your values requires you to identify what those values are. One way to do this is to reflect on life events that changed your life, whether positive or challenging, and think about what they revealed about what truly matters to you. For example, if you were offered a global opportunity to showcase your playwrighting talent, you accepted it because it would have helped to catapult your career to a new level. Your acceptance of this global opportunity shows you value exposure to a global audience, excellence, positive working relationships, meeting new people, collaboration, dreaming big, and creativity.

Another step in ensuring your actions align with your values is to reflect on why you want to say "yes." Your values must resonate with your inner beliefs that influence your behavior, daily habits, and decisions. For example, when life throws you lemons, what do you do? When life throws me lemons, I make lemonade that is organic, fair-trade, and I drink it in a reusable cup—because I value sustainability, environmental conservation, self-compassion, quality, and fairness. Personal values are principles that guide you, influence your decision-making, and reveal your true self.

If you notice a disconnection between your actions and values, know it is common. It can be annoying when what you intend to do does not align with what you did. For example, you value deep, meaningful connections, so you usually say "yes" to small gatherings with close friends but find yourself tagging along to a large, impersonal party to celebrate your best friend's birthday with them.

The misalignment can be caused by many things, such as an existential crisis, peer or societal pressures, old habits that die hard like people-pleasing, conformity, or self-awareness issues (NeuroLaunch Editorial Team, 2024). You can expect to experience significant negative consequences when your actions do not align with your values, such as stress, emotional turmoil, and an inner knowing that you are being inauthentic. Suppose you ever find yourself in this situation. In that case, you can use strategies to help align your actions with your values, such as establishing new goals, replacing bad habits with good ones, or even reevaluating specific aspects of your life.

Accountability is critical in aligning your actions with your values and can lead to greater happiness, satisfaction, and success. Remember to set up systems to help keep you accountable for creating the desired change. These can include daily journaling or regular check-ins with an accountability partner, such as a therapist. Always celebrate your progress along your journey, not perfection! And remember, even Wonder Woman needed a sidekick—so do not hesitate to enlist some help.

Cultivating Self-Trust and Inner Wisdom

Trusting yourself and listening to your instincts, which hold so much wisdom, can be transformative. Intuition is that gut feeling that you cannot ignore how right something feels or how strongly you are pulled toward something as if it is in your best interest or a sudden insight you receive. It is often accompanied by feelings of ease, excitement, or hope, making you feel grounded and relaxed. It is different from fear or anxiety, so it is vital to know the difference between the two. For example, if you feel tense or stressed about a decision because you want to avoid a negative outcome, take time to evaluate whether it is truly a genuine intuitive warning or just overthinking to compromise yourself to please others. Think of it as the difference between your inner Yoda and a caffeine-induced jitter.

Self-awareness is central to trusting yourself and distinguishing between intuition and fear or anxiety. Self-awareness helps you recognize and understand your thoughts, emotions, and quirky behaviors (Fleming, 2024). You can practice self-awareness through mindful meditations to become more aware of your thoughts, feelings, and bodily sensations; daily journaling can help you reflect on your behaviors and emotions; seeking honest feedback from trusted family members or friends about your actions can provide insight into things you might miss; and practicing gratitude can shift your mind from focusing on what is lacking in your life to what is abundant (Miller, 2020; Pederson, 2022).

When you are self-aware, you can quickly and clearly identify intuitive signals. For example, if you always have a sense of dread about a particular situation, it might be your intuition guiding you to reconsider your choices. Or maybe it is just your brain reminding you that you forgot to turn off the stove—again. The clarity that self-awareness brings allows you to focus on what truly matters, guiding you toward the right decisions and choices.

Creating a Personal Mission Statement

A personal mission statement is a concise statement that helps you to identify your values, goals, purpose, and what success means to you (Herrity, 2024). It can be used as a framework to make decisions and help you focus on achieving your long-term goals.

A personal mission statement has two elements: who you want to be and what you want to accomplish. Consider the qualities of the person you want to become. Reflect on questions such as:

- What is most important to me?

- What character strengths do I want to possess?

- How do I want others to perceive me?

Additionally, consider your biggest goals and the legacy you want to leave behind, both personally and professionally. Remember to dream big. Consider questions such as:

- What are my long-term and short-term goals?

- What do I want to achieve in life?

- What do I want my legacy to be?

Creating a personal mission statement can be beneficial for gaining clarity on who you are, what truly matters to you, and how you will accomplish your goals. It helps you make decisions aligned with your values and long-term goals. It also helps to hold you accountable for your long-term objectives (Scott, 2022). Also, you can use it to overcome your people-pleasing habits.

You can use a personal mission statement to define what you find acceptable and communicate these boundaries to others, make decisions that prioritize your well-being and align with your values, and stay true to yourself, even during difficult times. Doing so will shift your focus from the fear of rejection, abandonment, or the need for external validation to internal fulfillment. Breaking free from people-pleasing habits and living a more authentic life is like finally ditching those uncomfortable heels for a pair of comfy sneakers—you suddenly realize how much better life can be when you are not constantly trying to impress everyone else.

Interactive Element

Creating a personal mission statement can be a powerful way to set boundaries, prioritize self-care, and focus on your goals. Grab a pen and paper and take some time to write down a clear and concise mission statement that is motivational, exciting, and meaningful, which you will revisit along your journey. Be true to yourself, and remember, this is your journey.

Instructions

Step 1: Reflect on your values.

- Think about what truly matters to you.

- Write down a few key values, core beliefs, and principles that guide your life. For example:

  - well-being

  - happiness

  - growth

  - authenticity

  - self-worth

  - compassion

  - balance

  - joy

  - purpose

  - meaningful connections

Step 2: Identify your goals.

- Consider your long-term and short-term goals in your personal and professional life.

- List your main goals. For example:

  - I want to prioritize personal well-being and happiness.

- o I will set healthy boundaries to encourage personal growth and development.

- o I want to live authentically and confidently.

- o I will nurture my self-worth by pursuing personal dreams and to support my loved ones.

- o I will strive to balance personal needs with others' needs while creating a joyful and purposeful life and build meaningful connections.

Step 3: Define your purpose.

- Think about what gives your life meaning and purpose.

- Jot down your purpose in a few sentences. For example:

  - o to create a positive impact in my life and others

  - o to foster personal development and support loved ones along their journey

  - o to lead by example and motivate others to embrace their true selves

  - o to achieve personal fulfillment while being a source of support and compassion

  - o to live a balanced and fulfilling life while fostering strong relationships

Step 4: Combine your values, goals, and purpose.

- Take your values, goals, and purpose you have identified and combine them into a clear and concise statement.

- Aim for a personal mission statement that excites and motivates you. For example:

o My mission is to live an authentic, balanced, and fulfilling life by setting healthy boundaries, pursuing my dreams, and fostering strong relationships while supporting and caring for my loved ones and others.

Step 5: Revisit and revise.

- Regularly review your mission statement to ensure it remains relevant and inspiring along your boundary-setting journey.

- Do not be afraid to revise it as your values, goals, and purpose evolve.

This exercise encourages self-reflection and self-awareness, which are essential for building a fulfilling and balanced life. Regularly revisiting your mission statement ensures that you stay aligned with your aspirations and can adapt to changes in your life, ultimately leading to greater satisfaction and success.

In the next chapter, you will learn about practical strategies for breaking the people-pleasing cycle. Remember, transformation is a journey that starts with small steps every day. You will also learn practical steps to build confidence in making decisions. I will discuss practical strategies to identify your core values and priorities to guide your decision-making process. I will also discuss practical steps to improve your time management.

Additionally, there are self-care practices that you can incorporate into your daily routine to help you stay the course. No worries; I will not ask you to climb Mount Everest or swim with sharks—unless that is your thing!

Chapter Four
Baby Steps to Big Changes

"Your worth isn't measured by how many times you say yes when you want to say No"
-H.L Nakamura

Could you see yourself saying "no" to small requests in the future? Let me tell you a bit more about my story. I was the epitome of a people-pleaser, from staying late to help colleagues with their work to consistently supporting them in advancing their careers. However, this constant need to please others left me feeling exhausted, stressed, and underappreciated.

One day, after another sleepless night worrying about work, I decided I needed to change. I started to take sFmall steps, such as setting a simple work boundary: No more checking work emails after 6 p.m. At first, it felt strange and uncomfortable, but I stuck with it. Gradually, I noticed that this small change gave me more time to relax and recharge.

Encouraged by this success, I practiced saying "no" to small requests for which I did not have the time, interest, or energy to do. When a colleague asked me to take another work shift, I politely declined, explaining that I was already at capacity with my workload and could not squeeze another work shift into my schedule at our local county hospital. To my surprise, the world did not end, and my colleague understood.

As I continued to set small boundaries, I found that my anxiety and stress levels decreased, and I felt more in control of my life. I even enjoyed my work more, as I was no longer overwhelmed by trying to do everything for everyone.

My journey was not easy, but I could break free from my people-pleasing habits by starting small and gradually building my confidence. Today, I feel more balanced, fulfilled, and happy, knowing I can take good care of myself while still being a supportive colleague and friend.

Starting Small: Saying "No" to Minor Requests

Saying "no" can be challenging for people-pleasers, but practical strategies exist for breaking the people-pleasing cycle. Taking small steps is a surefire way to prioritize your needs and bring relief for both you and others.

Consider following the steps below to start saying "no" to minor requests. I have included specific examples of what you could say if a colleague asked you to take on an extra task at work.

1. **Acknowledge the request:** You want to start by politely acknowledging their request to demonstrate that their needs matter to you and that you have heard and understood their request. For example, you could say, "I appreciate you asking me," or "I have received your request." Think of it as the verbal equivalent of nodding your head vigorously during a Zoom call to show you are paying attention. It leaves the colleague

making the request feeling respected, validated, and important.

2. **Express appreciation for their trust:** After acknowledging the request, thank the person for considering you because it helps to maintain a respectful and positive tone. For instance, you could say, "Thank you for thinking of me for this," or "Thank you for reaching out to me about this." By saying this, you acknowledge their effort to communicate with you and show that you value their initiative. It is like saying, "Thanks for believing I have my life together enough to help you out," even if you are secretly juggling a million things.

3. **Explain why you cannot fulfill the request:** You need to briefly explain why you cannot help without over-explaining yourself. Your response will demonstrate that you value the person's request enough to provide a thoughtful response rather than giving a simple "no." It helps them see things from your perspective and appreciate your honesty. For example, with an assertive and decisive tone, you could say, "I am currently at capacity with my workload and cannot take on anything additional right now." Think of it as your polite way of saying, "My plate is full; it is practically a buffet."

4. **Offer an alternative:** After declining their request, consider suggesting an alternative solution or someone else you think can help them. Offering an alternative encourages collaboration, demonstrates your problem-solving skills, and that you are a team player who still wants to support them. For instance, you could say, "Since I am at capacity and cannot help with this

request, I think maybe Jeremy could assist you. What do you think about that?" It is like saying, "I cannot bake the cake, but I know a great bakery that can whip up something fabulous."

5. **Embrace self-validation:** When you say "no" to small requests, no one will come to validate that you made the right decision. So, you have to be the one to remind yourself that it is okay to say "no" to prioritize what you have going on in your life besides work; you must spend time with yourself and those who care about you. For example, tell yourself: "It is okay to prioritize my well-being and say "no" when I need to." Think of it as giving yourself a high-five in the mirror—because you deserve it! Self-validation is a concept I wish I had known about from a young age to reduce my anxiety and stress about pleasing everyone all the time. Along my journey, self-validation has helped me to boost my confidence in prioritizing my needs.

Building Confidence in Your Decisions

Building confidence in your decision-making process is a valuable skill. It can lead to intentional, fulfilling, and authentic choices like watering and watching a plant grow.

Here are practical steps to help build confidence in your decision-making process with clarity:

1. **Take a moment to gather your thoughts:** When you are faced with making a decision, pause and assess how you think and feel about the matter. You can take ten deep breaths to calm your mind and think more clearly. Think of it as hitting the reset button on your brain. Also, it is a great excuse to avoid making decisions while hangry.

2. **Gain clarity on your long-term vision:** Think about how this decision aligns with who you want to be and where you want to be. The dream life you picture for yourself, not the one where you are a superwoman, but the realistic one where you are happy and fulfilled, will

guide you in making choices consistent with your long-term vision.

3. **Avoid seeking excessive opinions:** You can rely on trusted individuals to seek wise counsel before deciding. However, as a people-pleaser, relying on others' opinions to seek their approval can lead to codependency, confusion, and indecision. Take small steps toward trusting your judgment about going to lunch with your friends, applying for a new leadership position, or going on that international business trip with your manager. Consider seeking external advice to broaden your perspective to make the best decision. Moreover, remember that too many cooks in the kitchen can spoil the broth.

4. **Listen to your intuition:** As previously discussed, your intuition is like a wise old friend who has seen it all. Trust it. If something feels off, it probably is, and you will regret going against your gut feelings and instincts. Our intuition is part of our subconscious that processes information using sensory input and past experiences. For instance, our subconscious mind can process around 11 million bits per second of sensory data, including everything we can see, hear, smell, taste, and touch, even when unaware of it (Sinn, 2020). Also, our subconscious mind serves as a vast archive of all our past experiences, memories, and learned behaviors. Your subconscious mind quickly and efficiently draws on past experiences and sensory input to guide you to the right choice.

5. **Create a pros and cons list:** Channel your inner detective and list the pros and cons. It is like solving a mystery where the culprit is the best decision. You will see the potential outcomes of your decision and assess

the best choice. Writing down the advantages and disadvantages of each choice makes the decision-making process more manageable and achievable.

6. **Focus on the process and growth:** There is a saying that goes: It is not about the destination but the journey. Instead of fixating on the final result, focus on the learning and growth opportunities that come with each decision to reduce the pressure and enjoy the process. Each decision is a step toward growth, even if it sometimes feels like you are stepping on Lego bricks.

7. **Commit to your decision with determination, not fear or anxiety:** Once you have decided, stick to your decision with the determination of a dog trying to push through a slightly opened door to get to their beloved owner. Fear and anxiety are just pesky mice trying to distract you and make you second-guess yourself. You should never feel uncertain of yourself after making a decision. Instead, you should feel positive that you made the right choice.

Identifying Your Core Values and Priorities

Your core values and priorities should resonate with your vision for your life and overall well-being. Below are seven practical steps to help you navigate this process.

1. **Self-reflection:** Take time to consider moments when you felt truly fulfilled and those when you felt disappointed. What values were present during those distinct moments? Think of it as a personal highlight

reel—minus the embarrassing fashion choices from the early 2000s.

2. **Self-coaching:** Ask yourself deep, meaningful questions such as "What will I never allow someone or anything to change my mind on?" "What qualities do I admire in others and why?" "What do I hope people will say about me when I am no longer here?"

3. **Brainstorming a list of potential values:** Write down any values that resonate with you. If that is difficult, consider visiting websites that provide comprehensive lists of values. As you write your list of values that speak to you, ask yourself: What is most important to me? Think of it as shopping for your soul—no credit card required.

4. **Narrowing down the list:** Once you have a comprehensive list, start narrowing it down to about 10 to 15 values. You can start by grouping similar values together and then selecting the one that best captures the essence of the group. It is like decluttering your closet. Keep the essentials and remove the "What was I thinking?" items.

5. **Prioritizing your values:** Which five of the values you narrowed down are the most important? These values should define who you are at this moment in time. Over time, you will change, and your prioritization of your values will evolve, too. Think of it as your top five playlist—these tracks define your life's soundtrack.

6. **Arranging your core values in order of importance:** Sort your top five core values from most to least important right now. Keep this list safe for future reference because it will guide your decision-making

process. It is like organizing your Netflix queue—prioritize what you cannot wait to watch.

7. **Reflect and revisit:** It is crucial to occasionally revisit your values and make changes when necessary as you evolve; this helps ensure your core values align with your authentic self and long-term vision. Like updating your wardrobe, ensuring your values still fit your current style.

Time Management for Recovering People-Pleasers

Improving your time management as a recovering people-pleaser is another good step to creating a more balanced, fulfilled, and authentic life. Here are eight steps you can follow to improve your time management:

1. **Establish boundaries:** This is your territory, your time. You have the power to decide what you can and cannot tolerate from others. Think of it as setting up a "No Trespassing" sign for your time. Then, communicate respectfully but firmly to let others know your boundaries when necessary; this is not about being rigid but about being in control.

2. **Make gradual behavioral changes:** Start saying "no" to small requests, and gradually, you will build the courage and confidence to decline larger requests; this is not about being confrontational; it is about setting yourself free. Practice assertiveness to communicate your needs effectively. Think of it as channeling your inner boss lady and stepping into a world of freedom.

3. **Focus on tasks aligned with your values and long-term vision:** Use the list of your core values from above to prioritize tasks that contribute to your long-term objectives. Imagine you are organizing your to-do list; keep what sparks joy and ditch the rest.

4. **Assess requests from others:** Do not hastily say "yes" to requests from others. Take your time to consider whether it aligns with your core values and priorities. Think of it as putting a "Please Hold" sign on your brain.

5. **Consider the impact of saying "yes" to requests:** While you are still toying with the idea of accepting or declining the request, consider evaluating the potential long-term effects saying "yes" might have on your time, resources, relationships, energy, and well-being. It is like deciding whether to add another scoop of ice cream—delicious but potentially regrettable.

6. **Be confident when saying "no":** Whenever you say "no" to something, be honest about your reasons and stay firm with your decision. Remember, you are not being mean; you are being a time-management ninja!

7. **Healthy relationships involve reciprocity:** Giving and receiving support, love, mutual respect, and understanding are crucial in relationships. Remember, your needs are as important as everyone else's. Think of it like a potluck—everyone brings a homemade food dish to the table, and nobody wants to be the one who only brings napkins.

8. **Become a cheerful helper:** Only offer to help someone when you genuinely want to help, not out of obligation, fear of rejection, or to seek others' approval. Helping others should come from the goodness of your

heart without pressure. Think of it as giving from a full cup, not an empty one.

Self-Care Practices to Support Your Journey

Self-care was challenging to incorporate into my daily routine because I got used to prioritizing other people and my work responsibilities before my physical, emotional, and mental needs. It would take me a health scare or feeling my physical, emotional, and mental reserves depleted to nurture myself. That is bad. Please do not be like this. Walking around your house for twenty minutes listening to your favorite songs or taking a bubble bath with droplets of essential oils is self-care. Developing these habits of taking time for yourself is excellent for your well-being, boosts your self-confidence, and helps you overcome seeking external validation (Kim, 2023).

Consider these practical steps for self-care practices that can help you stay the course, especially as a recovering people-pleaser.

1. **Set boundaries:** This will be discussed in the next chapter in greater detail.

2. **Celebrate small victories:** Celebrating small wins helps you to recognize and reward your progress and achievements. Therefore, it increases motivation, maintains momentum, and reinforces positive behavior. Think of it as giving yourself a gold star—because who does not love feeling like a kindergarten superstar?

3. **Engage in positive self-talk:** Think positively to reinforce your worth and capabilities. Listening and saying positive affirmations aloud to yourself can help build your self-esteem and resilience. Imagine you are your hype person, like a DJ at a party: "And now, give it up for the amazing, the incredible, YOU!"

4. **Set Specific, Measurable, Attainable, Relevant, and Time-bound (SMART) goals:** For each self-care practice you want to do, have clear goals for them to stay focused and monitor your progress. It is like setting up a GPS for your self-care journey—no more getting lost in the land of "I will do it later."

5. **Treat yourself:** Regularly show appreciation to yourself, regardless of progress and achievements, to maintain your well-being and happiness. You deserve it!

Interactive Element

Here is a comprehensive list of the practical steps to start small with recovering from your people-pleasing tendencies:

1. **Start saying "no" to minor requests.**

   a. Acknowledge requests to validate the person.

   b. Express appreciation for considering you.

   c. Give reasons for declining a request.

   d. Offer an alternative solution.

    e. Embrace self-validation for each decision you make.

2. **Build confidence in your decision-making.**

    a. Pause and gather your thoughts before deciding.

    b. Gain clarity on whether each decision is consistent with your long-term vision.

    c. Instead of seeking excessive opinions, seek wise counsel from a few trusted individuals.

    d. Pay attention to your gut feelings.

    e. Write a pros and cons list to make the decision-making process more manageable.

    f. Focus on growth and learning instead of the final result.

    g. Confidently stick to your decision.

3. **Identify your core values and priorities.**

    a. Consider the values present in moments when you felt truly fulfilled and those when you felt disappointed.

    b. Look within to identify your core values and priorities.

    c. Brainstorm a comprehensive list of potential values.

    d. Narrow down this list to about 10 to 15 values.

    e. Select the five most important values.

f. Arrange the top five values in order of importance.

g. Regularly reflect and revisit your values as you evolve.

4. **Improve your time management.**

a. Establish boundaries to be in control.

b. Make gradual behavioral changes.

c. Take on tasks aligned with your values and long-term objectives.

d. Evaluate requests from others.

e. Consider the long-term potential effects of saying "yes" to requests.

f. Be authentic and confident when saying "no."

g. Ensure your relationships have equal give and take.

h. Offer assistance when you genuinely want to.

5. **Prioritize self-care practices.**

a. Set boundaries.

b. Celebrate small wins.

c. Have positive thoughts to build your confidence.

d. Set SMART goals to remain focused.

e. Regularly treat yourself.

In the next chapter, I will delve into the concept of boundaries and their crucial role in mental health, relationships, and overall life satisfaction. I will also explore how boundaries influence self-esteem, stress management, and resilience. Remember, self-care is not a luxury but a necessity for overall well-being. I will discuss how saying "no" is not selfish; it is an act of self-care.

I will explore physical, emotional, time, and work boundaries and the benefits of setting boundaries. I will address common myths about setting boundaries by revealing the truth.

Rest assured that setting boundaries does not mean you will turn into a hermit living in a cave—unless that is your dream!

Bonus Content

Bonus Content:
A Special Gift Just for You!

As a thank you for investing in your personal growth, I'm excited to offer you a Self-Love Journal for Women!

The Complete Self-Love Journal for Women

This guide is designed to support your journey of self-compassion and reflection. It includes:

✦ 365 prompts to inspire daily reflection

✦ Focus topics to nurture different aspects of your well-being

Remember, self-love is a continuous journey, and each step you take is a powerful act of self-compassion and growth. Let this journal guide you, support you, and remind you of the incredible strength and beauty that resides within you.

SCAN ME☐

H.L. Nakamura, RN-BSN
Author, Owner of Radiant Beauty RN

Chapter Five
The Power of Saying "No"

"Continuous and habitual people-pleasing is like trying to fill others' cups while yours has a hole in the bottom" -Unknown

To illustrate healthy versus unhealthy boundaries, here are some scenarios:

Scenario	Unhealthy Boundaries	Healthy Boundaries
Social invitations	Sarah, in her late thirties, feels obligated to attend every social event she is invited to, even when she is exhausted or has other commitments.	Emma, also in her late thirties, understands the importance of self-care. She politely declines invitations when she needs rest or has other priorities.
Workplace demands	Lisa, in her early forties, struggles to say no to additional work assignments. She often stays late at the office, sacrificing her personal time and well-being.	Megan, also in her early forties, communicates her workload limits clearly to her boss and colleagues. She prioritizes tasks and delegates when necessary.

Family expectations	Anna, in her mid-thirties, feels pressured to meet her family's expectations, such as attending every family gathering or fulfilling every request for help.	Rachel, in her mid-thirties, sets clear boundaries with her family. She communicates her availability and limits, ensuring she has time for herself and her immediate family.
Personal relationships	Jessica, in her early forties, finds it difficult to express her needs and desires in her romantic relationship. She often goes along with her partner's wishes.	Laura, also in her early forties, openly communicates her needs and desires with her partner. They discuss and negotiate their preferences, ensuring both feel heard and respected.

Understanding Boundaries and Why They Matter

Boundaries are your limits about interactions and relationships. After identifying your limits, it is vital to set boundaries to protect your privacy and well-being. Additionally, assertively communicating your boundaries with people lets them know how you want to be treated. If they disrespect your boundaries, you can address the boundary violation by bringing it up to them, ideally within 72 hours before they forget. Be consistent in enforcing your boundaries because that helps people remember and respect them. You could also set consequences, for example, saying "no" to further requests or limiting contact. If you have a trustworthy friend, family member, or mental health professional, you could talk to them about the situation to get their advice on managing it. As a last resort, you can consider cutting the person or people off if the disrespect is egregious.

It can be challenging to set and maintain boundaries when you have never done that before. You might feel fearful, anxious, uncomfortable, or even conflict-averse when you know you should draw the line (*Boundaries*, n.d.). Boundaries protect our mental health by ensuring we do not become emotional sponges, soaking up feelings of resentment and frustration when people expect a lot of you, which can happen often. Boundaries in relationships prevent misunderstandings and disagreements that can create stress for all parties involved. Boundaries help you experience overall life satisfaction by allocating time and energy to different aspects of your life to build a more balanced life. Imagine juggling being a mom and a career woman without boundaries—sounds stressful, right? Generally speaking, erecting boundaries is a way to safeguard your mental health, personal space, feelings, and well-being.

Healthy boundaries can impact self-esteem. It is like giving yourself a daily dose of self-love. Every time you set and maintain boundaries, it positively affirms your self-worth and helps you put your needs first, which increases your self-confidence and self-respect (Streed, 2024). Setting boundaries is like having a personal bouncer who keeps stress at bay. When you effectively communicate your limits, you prevent taking on too much responsibility, feeling exhausted, and burnout, making life much less chaotic. Establishing boundaries will help enhance your resilience. As Edmund Hillary once said: "It is not the mountain we conquer, but ourselves (Quoteresearch, 2016)."

This quote means that it is not life's challenges we must overcome; it is our ability to handle what life throws and bounce back from adversity. In my own life, this quote means: It is not the requests people make, the interactions that leave you feeling discomfort, or relationships that drain your time, resources, and energy that we must conquer, but our ability to handle stress, conflict, fear of abandonment, failure, and rejection and bounce back from the consequences of people-pleasing that genuinely makes you resilient.

The Difference Between Selfishness and Self-Care

Selfishness is like being the star of your show, where you hog the spotlight and forget there is an audience. It is all about "me, myself, and I" without considering others' needs and well-being. Selfishness makes people think only about their needs and desires, disregarding the impact of their actions on those around them. Additionally, selfishness contradicts the saying: "No man is an island," because it reflects a drive for personal gain, ignoring the individuals who helped them thrive.

On the other hand, self-care is a practice that involves activities or simple rituals that replenish, re-energize, and rejuvenate your mind, body, spirit, and soul so that you can be the best version of yourself for yourself and others. Self-care helps you preserve or improve your health or well-being (*Understanding Selfishness vs. Self-Care,* 2020).

Self-care is essential for your health and well-being, and selfishness is not the same. Selfishness is like eating the last slice of pizza without asking if anyone else wants it. Self-care ensures you eat a well-balanced meal to have the energy to share that pizza with friends later.

Selfish people can be seen as "users" because they can take more than they give, exploit relationships to get what they want, and struggle to understand or care about the feelings and needs of others. Behaving in this manner can lead to disconnection and resentment from others, like when you binge-watch a series without your partner and spoil the ending. Conversely, practicing self-care can make others perceive you as a "giver" because when you fill up your cup, you can be more present in the moment, empathetic to people's needs, and supportive to those around you, like taking a nap so you do not turn into a grumpy cat.

In the long run, selfishness usually results in negative consequences for relationships, such as isolation, frequent conflicts, frustration, and lack of depth and authenticity. Selfishness can also have a long-term impact on personal growth, such as missing out on opportunities to learn from interactions and experiences with others on an emotional and social level. Additionally, selfishness can make one fail to see things from others' perspectives and miss out on engaging in valuable experiences and lessons with others. Over time, if you become someone known for your self-centeredness, people may not want to associate with you personally and professionally, like being the person who never shares their toys.

Self-care has numerous long-term effects on resilience. Self-care practices like exercise or picking flowers in the garden can help you manage stress levels, allow time and space to process your emotions healthily, and help you develop effective coping mechanisms. Also, your self-care routine can include many activities that will help improve your physical health and longevity, such as drinking enough water, attending regular medical checkups, cleansing your gut, getting the minerals and vitamins your body needs, and eating a well-balanced diet. To improve your mental health, engaging in activities that encourage you to spend time in nature, for example, can help reduce anxiety and depression.

Moreover, self-care enriches relationships. When you practice self-care, you are more likely to communicate effectively and empathetically with others. You have the energy and mental clarity to spend quality time with loved ones, and you set healthy boundaries. This is akin to a friend who always has a smile and a kind word, making them a joy to be around. By prioritizing self-care, you can be that friend, enriching your relationships and enhancing your well-being.

Saying "no" can be a powerful act of self-care, not selfishness. When you say "no," you conserve your energy for what truly matters, like saving your phone battery for important calls instead of draining it on endless cat videos. You also manage your workload better and reduce stress levels, which helps you avoid turning into a stress-zilla. Moreover, saying "no" keeps you focused on your goals and priorities so that you are less likely to get sidetracked by shiny objects or the latest TikTok dance craze. It is about setting healthy boundaries and managing your energy for maximum effectiveness and well-being.

Types of Boundaries: Physical, Emotional, Time and Work

Physical boundaries are like the invisible force fields we wish we had in crowded elevators. Examples of physical boundaries include personal space and physical comfort. Personal space refers to the physical space around your body that you would not feel comfortable with someone invading without your permission. Physical comfort refers to feeling at ease with physical touch and proximity (*15 Types of Healthy Boundaries*, n.d.). Another example is personal privacy. For instance, you may have a boundary about not allowing people to open the door without knocking in your room, or you may not share personal items like your phone with anyone.

Emotional boundaries are equivalent to not letting someone borrow your favorite sweater. Emotional boundaries involve drawing the line between how much emotional energy you are willing to give within relationships and protecting your feelings, thoughts, and emotional needs. Emotional boundaries help us to communicate our limits and expectations, express our emotions, say "no" with no guilt, and not take on the feelings, needs, or problems of others. Moreover, they help us share others' feelings and listen to them without judgment, feeling overwhelmed, or losing ourselves.

Time boundaries are like finding a matching pair of socks in a laundry basket—challenging but incredibly satisfying when you get it right. They refer to setting realistic expectations by using time wisely and learning to say "no" to overcommitting yourself because you value your time. The relief of saying "no" can be liberating and stress-releasing and helps you manage time commitments better. By prioritizing tasks in order of importance and urgency and using strategies such as time blocking, you can allocate specific periods for different tasks or activities, thereby maintaining a work-life balance.

You can achieve a work-life balance, but it will require practice and patience with yourself. You must set clear limits on your availability for work-related tasks and ensure you have the time allocated for fun, calming activities that put a spring in your step. These self-care activities are not a luxury but necessary to prevent burnout and show yourself love and appreciation. So, set time aside to schedule a date with yourself, and make it a priority.

The Benefits of Setting Boundaries

Setting boundaries can enhance the quality of our relationships and help us grow and earn people's respect. Here are ten benefits of setting boundaries:

- Setting boundaries encourages self-discipline. When you value your time, you will limit people who waste your time and minimize distractions, which helps you become more productive and focused.

- When someone sets boundaries with you, you are accepting of them and experience little to no anger or resentment toward them. After all, who has time for drama when you can respect each other's space?

- Even though you know people may not respect a boundary you set, verbalizing your boundaries can help you honor your limits. You have more time and energy to focus on your needs and wants than on others' needs and wants, contributing to a sense of peace and stability.

- You respect yourself more for prioritizing your needs above others, and others automatically respect you for setting a boundary. It is a win-win—like getting the last scoop of ice cream and not feeling guilty about it.

- In relationships, drawing the line about what they can and should not expect from you fosters harmony between you and others. When you firmly communicate your boundaries and live them publicly, you can quickly identify toxic relationships and reassess them if disrespect persists.

- Boundaries turn you into a positive role model. Setting your boundaries and upholding them with others inspires others to do the same in their relationships. It is like starting a positive chain reaction, one boundary at a time.

- As you set and maintain boundaries, your self-esteem will increase. You will realize that your self-worth should not be based on what you can provide or do for others, but it should be based on your talents and gifts. Each time you communicate your boundaries, you become more confident and empowered. It is like leveling up after a breakup—each boundary strengthens you.

- Stating clear boundaries ensures no misunderstandings when people ask you to explain or defend them, reducing stress and anxiety. The more you practice communicating your boundaries, the more your stress and anxiety decrease, providing a sense of control and autonomy in your life.

- Setting clear boundaries helps others to understand you better and accept you more. Boundaries reflect our sense of self and values; when people see what you value, they know who you are. It is like giving people a roadmap to the real you.

Common Boundary Myths Debunked

Setting boundaries often gets a bad rap, but I will clear up some common misconceptions and show you how it can positively impact your personal well-being and relationships.

- **Boundaries are selfish:** As previously discussed, boundaries allow you to take care of your needs and feel in charge while being there for others when you want to; it is not an act of selfishness.

- **Boundaries are negative and toxic**: Everyone deserves to create healthy interactions, situations, relationships, and spaces with others where they can feel safe, heard, and seen. In turn, boundaries can do this and ultimately benefit everyone involved. It is like installing a good antivirus on your computer—it keeps the bad stuff out and lets the good stuff in, just like boundaries keep negativity and toxicity out and allow positivity and wholesomeness into your life.

- **Boundaries make you rude:** When you no longer accept being everyone's doormat and decide to set boundaries and maintain them, some people may take that the wrong way. However, being honest and straightforward about your limits does not make you rude. It helps to eliminate confusion and resentment in relationships. Think of it as upgrading from a doormat to a welcome mat—still friendly, but with clear limits.

- **Boundaries hurt relationships:** Boundaries help improve communication because they foster mutual respect and understanding, and you learn to value and accept each other. It is like setting the rules for a board game—everyone knows what to expect, and the game runs smoothly without arguments.

- **Setting boundaries is too much work:** As with any skill set, it can be daunting at first, but practice makes perfect. Setting boundaries at first can be challenging, but with practice, you will set boundaries with ease, confidence, and compassion. You will realize that what is too hard is the dysfunction, discomfort, sometimes abuse and manipulation, conflict, and hatred caused by tolerating behavior that you should not have from the get-go.

Interactive Element

This short quiz can help you assess your current boundary-setting habits across different types of boundaries.

Grab a pen and paper (or your favorite digital device) and see how you score!

Boundary-Setting Habits Quiz

Physical Boundaries

- How comfortable are you with physical touch from others (e.g., hugs, handshakes)?

    o Very comfortable, I do not mind at all.

    o Comfortable, but only with people I know well.

    o Uncomfortable, I prefer minimal physical contact.

    o Very uncomfortable, I avoid physical contact whenever possible.

- Do you feel your personal space is respected by others?

    o Always

    o Most of the time

    o Sometimes

    o Rarely

Emotional Boundaries

- How often do you share your personal feelings and thoughts with others?

    o Frequently, with anyone who asks.

    o Often, but only with close friends and family.

○ Occasionally, and only with a few trusted people.

○ Rarely, I keep my feelings to myself.

- Do you feel emotionally drained after interacting with certain people?

    ○ Never

    ○ Rarely

    ○ Sometimes

    ○ Often

Time Boundaries

- How do you manage your time when others ask for your help?

    ○ I always say yes, even if it disrupts my schedule.

    ○ I usually say yes but try to manage my time.

    ○ I sometimes say no, depending on my availability.

    ○ I often say no to protect my time.

- Do you feel you have enough time for yourself and your interests?

    ○ Always

    ○ Most of the time

    ○ Sometimes

    ○ Rarely

Work Boundaries

- How do you handle work-related requests outside of your working hours?

  o I always respond, no matter the time.

  o I usually respond but try to set limits.

  o I sometimes respond, depending on the urgency.

  o I rarely respond, I protect my personal time.

- Do you feel your workload is manageable and respects your personal boundaries?

  o Always

  o Most of the time

  o Sometimes

  o Rarely

Scoring

- **Mostly As**: You might need to work on setting stronger boundaries. Remember, it is okay to say no and prioritize your well-being.

- **Mostly Bs**: You have a good sense of boundaries but could benefit from being more assertive in certain areas.

- **Mostly Cs**: You are fairly balanced in setting boundaries but might need to fine-tune them to better protect your time and energy.

- **Mostly Ds**: You have strong boundaries in place. Keep up the good work and continue to prioritize your needs.

In the next chapter, you will learn about self-concept and how to redefine yours. Do not fret; redefining your self-concept does not mean you must adopt a new identity and disappear to a deserted island—unless that is on your bucket list!

I will provide advice on how to challenge limiting beliefs. I will discuss the importance of reclaiming one's agency over one's life and highlight the value of setting boundaries and saying "no." You will also learn about assertiveness techniques.

Setbacks are an inevitable part of growth and transformation. I will provide coping mechanisms for handling relapses, such as resilience strategies and reframing setbacks as learning curves. I will also discuss the importance of acknowledging and appreciating incremental progress. I will also offer examples of simple ways to celebrate milestones.

I will explore the impact boundary-setting can have on others, especially in relationships where you model healthy boundaries to them.

Chapter Six
Rewriting Your Story

*"When you try to be everything to everyone,
you end up being a stranger to yourself" --
Unknown*

I n the early stages of my transformation journey of moving away from being a people-pleaser, I always would ask myself, "Could I go from being everyone's 'yes-woman' to the 'author of my own life'?" At the back of my mind, I always knew there was a possibility of change or transformation because of my desire, vision, ambition, and determination to shift from a passive role as the "yes-woman" to an empowered one where I was the author of my life. Let us continue on this journey to achieving personal growth and transformation.

Creating a New Narrative Around Your Identity

Self-concept refers to our knowledge of ourselves, which encompasses who we are physically, socially, and personally, as well as our beliefs, attributes, behaviors, and abilities (Ackerman, 2018; Cherry, 2024b). When redefining your self-concept, you need to ask yourself: "Who am I?" To answer this question, you will need to draw from social interactions, past experiences, and self-reflections because our self-concept is influenced by these factors (Ackerman, 2018).

Carl Rogers' self-concept theory has three components: Self-image, self-esteem, and ideal self (Vinney, 2024). Self-image refers to your knowledge about yourself—your physicality, social roles, and unique traits. Your self-image can be inflated, especially if you hold one or more personal traits in high regard and others in a negative regard. Think of it as your personal highlight reel, but sometimes with a few bloopers.

Self-esteem heavily relies on self-evaluations. It is usually based on your comparisons with others and how they respond. When people have high self-esteem, it usually stems from realizing they are better at something than others, and people react well to their talents, gifts, or abilities, and their self-esteem grows in that area. Conversely, low self-esteem can stem from feeling inadequate in one or more areas compared to others, and people respond unfavorably to what they do, which can plummet their self-esteem. It is normal to be a rock star in one area ("I am a good aunt") and a karaoke nightmare in another ("I am not a great singer").

The ideal self is the idea or mental image of who you want to be. One's self-image and ideal self usually do not match, which can negatively affect one's self-esteem. When your self-image and ideal self are similar or overlap a lot, it is known as congruence. It is best to have greater congruence because it allows you to feel more aligned with who you want to be, which helps you reach self-actualization. When there is a significant difference between your self-image and ideal self, this is called incongruence. Greater incongruence can cause internal conflict and confusion, making reaching self-actualization harder. It is like squeezing into a pair of shoes that are two sizes too small; it's frustrating and often impossible.

Redefining your self-concept is possible because it can change. The impact that our environment, people, and even medical diagnoses have on us can contribute to changing our self-concept. The sentimental value we put on places, the people in leadership roles in our lives, and medical diagnoses can help us understand why we think, feel, or behave in the way we do.

You can follow these steps to redefine your self-concept:

1. Start by examining your current self-concept. You can ask yourself: "What positive and negative beliefs do I hold about myself?" Be honest and consider various aspects of your life.

2. Identify the negative and self-critical beliefs that are holding you back.

3. Challenge your limiting beliefs about yourself by questioning the validity of those beliefs. You can ask yourself questions such as "What evidence do I have for this belief?" and "What would I rather believe?" You will realize these beliefs are based on past experiences or external opinions rather than facts.

4. To boost your self-worth, swap out your negative limiting beliefs for ones that empower and uplift you.

5. Imagine the person you want to be. Visualize the qualities you want to have and how you behave as your ideal self. Visualization is a powerful tool that can help bridge the gap between your self-image and your ideal self.

6. Take small, consistent actions that align with your new self-concept.

Besides questioning the validity of limiting beliefs, you can collect evidence that contradicts your limiting beliefs. As the saying goes: "Seeing is believing." Evidence such as receiving positive feedback and achieving success can vigorously challenge and change your limiting beliefs. You can also use positive affirmations to reinforce your new beliefs daily to ingrain them into your psyche. Additionally, surround yourself with supportive, loving people who encourage growth and challenge negative self-talk.

Let me share a personal story to illustrate this process. A few years before I went to college to become a registered nurse, I struggled with the belief that I was not good enough to pursue a career in nursing. This belief stemmed from not believing in my capabilities from a young age. However, I challenged this belief by writing down positive comments I received from people I have helped through my volunteerism and by looking at my academic accomplishments. Over time, I replaced my limiting belief with the empowering thought, "I am capable of becoming a registered nurse who can grow in the medical profession." This shift in mindset allowed me to pursue my passion and eventually start my medical spa.

Embracing the Role of the Empowered Decision-Maker

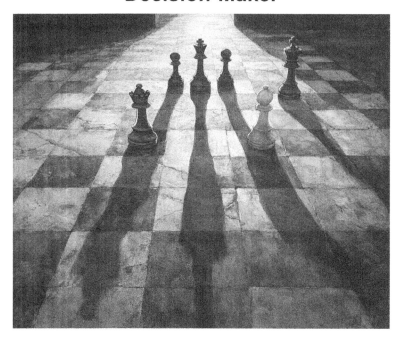

To rewrite your story, you must reclaim your agency, which means taking control of your life and decisions rather than allowing others to dictate your actions. Think of it as grabbing the remote control of your life and changing the channel from "Everyone Else's Demands" to "My Awesome Journey." To reclaim your agency, you must recognize that you have the power to shape your own experiences and outcomes. It also plays a crucial role in ensuring your well-being and achieving self-confidence.

Setting boundaries and learning to say "no" are essential to reclaiming your agency. These components' value lies in their acts of self-preservation and empowerment. The freedom to take charge of your life and make decisions for yourself is not a mere privilege but a responsibility you owe yourself. Setting boundaries and saying "no" is a declaration of self-respect by recognizing that your time and energy are precious and you deserve kindness and care. It is like saying, "I am worth it," with a confident hair flip. It is a testament that you take pride in yourself, and your boundaries are essential for safeguarding your self-esteem, self-confidence, and well-being.

Setting boundaries and saying "no" is a powerful tool to assert your autonomy and communicate where you draw the line in your relationships. You must actively shape the dynamics of your relationships to establish a precedent for being considerate of one another and equally giving and receiving between you and others. It is like being the director of your movie, ensuring everyone knows their role and respects the script.

We show others how to treat us by maintaining healthy boundaries and not accepting behavior that disrespects our dignity or diminishes our self-worth. By modeling this behavior, you will always foster genuinely respectful and mutually beneficial relationships where both parties feel appreciated and heard. It is like teaching others the golden rule: Treat me as I treat myself—with respect and a sprinkle of sass.

As we have previously discussed, setting boundaries and saying "no" is an act of self-care and self-compassion. Practicing self-care and self-compassion rejects the widespread idea that your worth as a people-pleaser depends on your ability to fulfill the needs and desires of others above your own. When you honor and prioritize your needs and desires, you reclaim agency over your life and stop neglecting yourself. It is like ensuring your phone is charged before you help someone else find a charger.

Setting boundaries and saying "no" eventually evolves into a powerful declaration of self-affirmation; it's a statement that acknowledges your needs are essential, your voice deserves to be heard, and your path to personal fulfillment is uncompromisable. It is like standing on a mountaintop and shouting, "I matter!"

I have briefly touched on assertiveness and two assertiveness techniques in Chapter 3: Using "I" statements to frame your thoughts and feelings from your perspective and speaking in a firm but respectful tone to appear confident. Here are other assertiveness techniques that can help you be more assertive to others:

- **Active listening:** Listen attentively to the message the other person is conveying to you and try to see things from their perspective. You will usually nod, paraphrase, and ask clarifying questions to show that you are paying attention. It is like being a detective but for feelings. Also, it helps you to communicate respectfully and effectively.

- **The fogging technique:** This approach acknowledges the other person's emotions while not giving them any reason to engage in a conflict or confrontational situation with you. For example, if someone expresses anger towards you, you can say, "I can see you are upset. Can we talk about what has made you upset in a calm manner?" It is like being a calm, collected superhero in the face of conflict.

- **Remain resolute:** Stay calm and firm if someone disrespects you or gives you pushback. Reiterate your point if needed and remain resolute without being aggressive. It is like being a rock in a storm—steady and unmovable.

Overcoming Setbacks and Dealing With Relapses

Let me share my story about overcoming a setback I experienced. When opening the medical spa, I meticulously planned every detail, from the decor to the advanced medical treatments. However, two weeks before the opening, I faced an unexpected setback—a crucial piece of medical equipment was delayed due to shipping issues. This delay threatened to derail my entire launch.

Initially, I felt overwhelmed and defeated. However, instead of letting this setback define me as a failure, I viewed it as a learning opportunity. I took a step back, reassessed my situation, and sought advice from my mentors and team. I identified alternative solutions through this process, such as renting equipment temporarily and rescheduling some appointments. My resilience and willingness to adapt helped me navigate the crisis and led to a successful and well-received opening. My ability to turn this potential disaster into a triumph became a defining moment in my entrepreneurial journey.

Setbacks are an inevitable part of growth and transformation. Here are some effective coping mechanisms to help you handle them.

- **Reframe setbacks as learning curves:** Whenever you experience setbacks, view them as opportunities to learn and grow. As my grandmother would say, "This too shall pass." When she would say this to me, I knew not to spend much time blaming myself and worrying about the setbacks because it was futile. All I could do was to extract valuable lessons and insights from the experience and apply them in the future. Also, every setback is a setup for a comeback, as they say.

- **Develop resilience strategies:** You can practice self-compassion. I will discuss this in detail in the last chapter. I cannot stress this enough: Surround yourself with a support network because they are a valuable source of free therapy and snacks! Along your journey, continue to embrace change and be willing to adapt your plans as needed. Staying flexible and adaptable will help you navigate challenges more effectively. It is like being a human rubber band—stretchy but resilient!

- **Create a relapse prevention plan:** Identify anything that might trigger you and develop strategies to avoid or manage them. A strategic coping plan can help you stay on track and prevent future relapses. It is like having a roadmap to navigate the twists and turns of life.

Celebrating Your Progress and Victories

As a successful person, you have learned to acknowledge and appreciate the incremental progress you made along the road to success. You can be either intrinsically or extrinsically motivated to keep going. Each win, whether small or big, can reinforce your belief in your capabilities, and celebrating your progress after tackling challenges fosters a winning mentality, and your brain releases those delightful endorphins that increase your happiness. This celebration encourages you to continue working hard to reach bigger goals long-term and tackle more significant challenges with grace, strategic thinking, and self-compassion. So, go ahead and give yourself a pat on the back (or a high five in the mirror)—you have earned it! Moreover, remember, every step forward, no matter how small, is a step in the right direction.

Here are some questions you can consider asking yourself to recognize the small achievements you have reached. It is easy not to notice small wins when you have your eye on achieving the larger goal.

- What small steps have you taken? Reflect on the minor actions you have taken towards your goals.

- What significant changes have you made? Consider the larger shifts in your behavior or mindset.

- How have you prioritized your needs recently? Think about the ways you have put your needs first.

Here are simple ways you can celebrate milestones.:

- You can use the questions above to journal your reflections about your small wins, including how the win made you feel. Journaling can help you internalize the positive impact of your progress, like the euphoria of finding that one missing sock in the laundry.

- Share the news about your small wins with people who supported you to reach your success. Their positive reactions can amplify your euphoria and provide additional support moving forward.

- Create a small trophy or certificate for your accomplishments or add a sticker to a progress chart. Visual reminders can bring you back to the moments of your milestones and victories, thus motivating you to go full throttle. Think of it as your personal Hall of Fame, minus the paparazzi.

- Pamper yourself with a spa day at home or at your favorite spa, and get a manicure, pedicure, massage, or other treatments. If you want to make it luxurious, have a glass of champagne.

- Take as many photos as possible of your wins to reminisce about in the future. It is another excellent way to document and remember your progress. You will thank yourself for the #ThrowbackThursday content.

Paying It Forward: Helping Others Set Boundaries

Sometimes, in relationships, when you prioritize your needs and assert your boundaries, people fear they will lose respect from others, or the relationship will become as tense as a cat in a room full of rocking chairs. Instead, stating and prioritizing your needs and asserting boundaries has far more positive, long-lasting effects. Stating and prioritizing needs and asserting boundaries can equalize the power dynamics between individuals. When both individuals do the same, they contribute equally to the terms and conditions of a respectful, healthy relationship. Healthy boundaries always maintain a good connection between individuals who want to make it work. Society should model boundary setting more as an act that works in the favor of all parties involved. Thus, more people will understand one another and honor their boundaries.

I encourage you to share your experiences and insights with loved ones to foster a supportive community. After all, a well-placed boundary is like a good fence—it makes for great neighbors and even better relationships!

Interactive Element

It's time to dive into this transformative exercise to rewrite your story! Grab a pen and paper and let us get started.

Instructions

1. Jot down the narratives you currently tell yourself. These might be thoughts or beliefs that influence your behavior, especially around people-pleasing. For example:

- "I must always be available for others."

- "If I say no, people will think I am selfish."

- "My needs are not as important as others'."

2. Rewrite these narratives into more empowering and self-supportive statements. This helps shift your mindset towards self-care and healthy boundaries. For example:

- "It is okay to prioritize my own needs."

- "Saying no is a form of self-respect."

- "I deserve to take care of myself just as much as I care for others."

3. Create a relapse prevention plan for when old habits resurface. Identify specific actions you can take to reinforce your new narratives. Here are some strategies:

- **Pause and reflect**: When you feel the urge to please, take a moment to breathe and reflect on your new narratives.

- **Set clear boundaries**: Practice saying "no" in a kind but firm manner. For example, "I appreciate you thinking of me, but I cannot commit to that right now."

- **Seek support**: Talk to a friend or therapist about your progress and challenges. They can offer encouragement and accountability.

Example

Let us put this into practice with an example:

1. Current narrative: "I need to make everyone happy."

2. Empowering alternative: "My happiness matters too."

3. Relapse prevention plan:

- **Pause and reflect**: When you feel the urge to please others, take a moment to breathe and remind yourself, "My happiness matters too."

- **Set clear boundaries**: Politely say, "Thank you for considering me, but I need to focus on my own well-being right now."

- **Seek support**: Talk to a trusted friend or mentor who can encourage you to prioritize your needs and offer guidance.

By consistently practicing these steps, you will gradually shift from people-pleasing to self-care, creating a healthier and more balanced life.

In the next chapter, you will gain practical advice on saying "no" gracefully and effectively and you will receive communication tips. I will provide scripts and phrases for saying "no" in everyday situations with friends, family, and coworkers. I will discuss how physical distance and tone, pitch, and volume variations convey personal boundaries, emotions, and support.

I will offer practical tips on saying "no" in professional settings to maintain boundaries and prioritize your well-being without burning bridges. I will also provide practical tips on saying "no" in personal relationships to strengthen relationships and empower yourself.

Chapter Seven
Crafting the Perfect "No"

S aying "no" is like planting a seed—as you nurture it, it will grow into a flourishing plant. When you say "no," you initially feel uncomfortable, but you blossom into a strong and empowered recovering people-pleaser with consistency. Are you excited to go through techniques for saying "no" gracefully and effectively in different contexts and learn practical communication tips?

Techniques for Saying "No" Gracefully

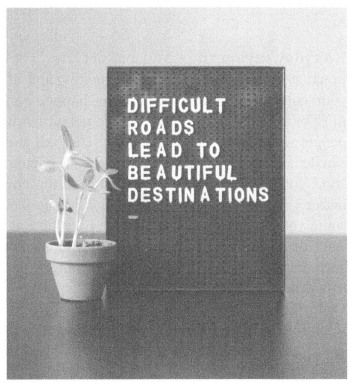

Many of us could use advice to help us be more assertive in our day-to-day interactions and relationships. However, learning how to gracefully and effectively say "no" is a lifelong journey. You can use these communication tips to get started:

- **Replace "no" with "later."** If you do not feel confident yet to say "no," make your automatic response to all requests, "Let me get back to you." It makes it easier. For instance, if you are at work, ask people to send you an email of their request so that you can get back to them without forgetting to do so. You can decline their request when they send the email and give a simple reason. You cannot rely on saying, "let me get back to you," forever. Saying "let me get back to you," repeatedly will make you come across as untrustworthy in the long term. Also, never lie about wanting to say "no." Honesty is the best policy, even if it feels like ripping off a Band-Aid.

- **Roleplay saying "no."** You may not always be able to practice saying "no" to requests, invites, and offers at your convenience. These situations happen randomly most of the time, and if they occur in person, sometimes people want an immediate answer. The best thing you can do is prepare for such situations by practicing saying "no." You can practice some "no" lines in the mirror or, better yet, get a trusted friend or family member to do some roleplaying with you. You can try finding polite ways of saying "no" to strangers in different contexts, such as waiters or waitresses, promoters, cashiers, colleagues, and other situations. Also, practice feeling comfortable with silence. Before responding, intentionally wait for a few good seconds. It will help make you appear sure of yourself and reduce that urge to please. Think of it as your dramatic pause—channel your inner Shakespeare!

- **Rely on your body language to assist with saying "no."** Approximately 65 to 90 percent of communication is through non-verbal cues (Van Edwards, 2024b). Here are three ways you can use your body language to signal "no." You could turn your torso away from the direction of the person making the request. You can also cross your arms to stop the conversation from moving forward. This posture is naturally defensive and not a nice one that we use when we feel reluctant about something. Additionally, you could turn your toes away to signal that you are uninterested. Our toes usually point in the direction we want to go, so when they are facing elsewhere, the person will get the message nonverbally. If you have difficulty saying "no," let your body do the talking—just do not start moonwalking away from the conversation!

- **Be assertive but graceful.** Gracefulness is an art of communication that conveys gentleness in the delivery, tone, and intention behind our words and actions. Eventually, I realized it was not about what you say but how you say it. I learned the power of a gentle touch on the arm, a kind smile, or a thoughtful pause before politely saying "no" can convey empathy and understanding, ensuring that all my interactions leave others feeling valued and respected. Practice using subtle gestures and exuding warmth in your voice to come across as graceful when saying "no." Think of it as adding a touch of elegance to your assertiveness—like saying "no" with a top hat and monocle.

Scripts and Phrases to Use in Different Situations

Here are more than 20 phrases of saying "no" with grace and lightheartedness you can use to help navigate various situations with friends, family, and coworkers.

- **With friends:**

  - I would love to, but I already have plans with my couch and a good book.

  - Thanks for inviting me, but I need some downtime today. My Netflix queue is feeling neglected.

  - That sounds like fun, but I cannot make it this time. My plants need me.

  - I wish I could join you, but I have other commitments, such as pretending to be an adult.

  - I am flattered you thought of me, but I must pass. My cat has scheduled a critical nap on my lap.

  - I am trying to cut back on my social calendar, so I must say "no." My social battery is running on empty.

  - I am honored, but I need to recharge my batteries. Moreover, by batteries, I mean my phone.

  - I am on a "no" streak right now, but thanks for asking! I am trying to set a world record.

○ Nice suggestion! Let me marinate on that for a bit, and I will get back to you.

- **With family:**

  ○ I appreciate the offer, but I cannot make it. I have got a date with my bed.

  ○ I would love to help, but I am swamped right now. My to-do list is plotting against me.

  ○ I cannot commit to that but thank you for thinking of me. I am currently in a committed relationship with my workload.

  ○ I have too much on my plate at the moment. Moreover, I am not just talking about dinner.

  ○ I must check with my better half to see if we have top-secret plans.

  ○ I am focusing on some personal projects and cannot take on anything else, such as perfecting my procrastination skills.

  ○ I need to prioritize my own needs right now. Self-care is calling my name, and it is very persuasive.

  ○ I am taking a break from extra responsibilities. My superhero cape is at the dry cleaners.

  ○ I am trying to simplify my schedule, so I must decline. My calendar is starting to look like a game of Tetris.

- **With coworkers:**

  o I appreciate the opportunity but cannot take on any more tasks. My brain is currently at full capacity.

  o I am currently working on a task and will be able to assist with only this one. My multitasking skills have reached their limit.

  o I would love to help, but my schedule is packed. My planner is giving me the side-eye.

  o I am not the best person for this task, but another colleague could help. Right now, I am more of a "cheerleader from the sidelines" kind of person.

  o I am honored that you asked, but I have to decline. My to-do list is starting to look like a novel.

  o I am focusing on my current projects and cannot take on more. My desk is already a disaster zone.

  o I am at capacity right now but thank you for considering me. My brain is currently buffering.

  o Let me consult my calendar and see if it approves of this. I will get back to you later.

  o I am not able to give this the attention it deserves. My attention span is on a coffee break.

Body Language and Tone: Nonverbal Communication of Boundaries

To pick up on this conversation from earlier on, body language and saying "no" physical distance can play a critical role in nonverbal communication. The amount of physical distance between you and others is known as proxemics (*Proxemics,* n.d.). The physical distance between yourself and others can communicate comfort level, intimacy, and formality. With people you are close with and love, you will typically have a distance of zero to eighteen inches between yourself and them. The distance between family members and friends can range from eighteen inches to four feet, signaling comfort. In social and professional settings, you are most likely to have a physical distance between four to ten feet that shows formality or a desire for personal space. The physical distance between people in public spaces is usually over 10 feet.

It is like having an invisible hula hoop around you—some people are allowed inside, while others need to admire your moves from a respectful distance.

Another critical aspect of nonverbal communication is tone. The way you speak can convey personal boundaries, emotions, and support. A soothing tone, for example, can convey gracefulness, ease, and compassion, while a sharp tone can express dissatisfaction, frustration, or anger. A welcoming and warm tone, on the other hand, can show support and empathy, making the listener feel valued and heard, much like a barista who remembers your coffee order.

Variations in pitch can be used to emphasize and express emotions. Using a higher pitch can denote excitement, joy, enthusiasm, or surprise. Conversely, using a lower pitch can indicate professionalism, seriousness, confidence, or calmness to people. Think of it as your "I have got this under control" voice.

Volume is another essential aspect of nonverbal communication; how you speak, whether softly or loudly, can convey different messages. Speaking softly to people can create a sense of intimacy and confidentiality. At the same time, a louder voice can command attention and authority or indicate urgency—perfect for announcing that the office cake is ready.

Saying "No" in Professional Settings

In a professional setting, the ability to say "no" politely is a key skill that maintains harmonious relationships with colleagues, clients, and guests and underscores the value of these connections. It is a demonstration of professional conduct that sets clear boundaries while respecting the needs of others.

Assertively and politely saying "no" to requests in the workplace is a powerful tool. It is not just about setting boundaries but also about preventing confusion, miscommunication, and conflict. Your words can shape a positive, constructive, and peaceful work environment and atmosphere, much like in personal relationships.

Mastering the art of assertive and polite refusals is more than just saying "no." It is a powerful demonstration of your effective communication skills and your respect and consideration for others in the workplace.

You maintain your boundaries by assertively and politely saying "no," making you more credible and reputable. It signals that you understand your role and responsibilities well and believe in your capabilities.

Furthermore, by standing your ground gracefully, you can earn respect from your coworkers and bosses and build rapport with clients.

So, let us dive into practical tips for saying "no" in the workplace that will help you navigate various situations.

1. Refrain from beating around the bush; respond as soon as possible to let the person know where you stand. Setting a precedent by stating your boundaries so people can understand is always a good idea. Consider it as

setting the stage for future interactions—clear and respectful.

2. Frame your refusal with positivity and appreciation to show you regret not being able to help them and thank them for thinking of you to let them down softly using words such as "Thanks for considering me, but I wish I could" or "While I am buried under my workload now..." It is like saying, "It is not you; it is me," but in a professional way.

3. Provide context about declining their request. It could be your workload, other matters taking more precedence, or clashing engagements or schedules making you say "no." A little transparency goes a long way. Also, it shows you are not just saying "no" because you are binge-watching your favorite series.

4. After providing context, you can propose solutions, options, or people to approach. Moreover, you can offer compromises if you feel comfortable with that. For example, a colleague asks you to help with a report due next week, and you genuinely do not have time to assist them. You might offer a compromise such as, "I wish I could dive in fully, but my schedule is packed this week. However, I can spare an hour to review your draft and give you feedback tomorrow. Would that help?" When you offer a compromise, you do not take on too much responsibility; instead, you offer valuable assistance within your capacity. It is like saying, "I cannot bake the whole cake, but I can help with the icing!" In this way, you are willing to help while maintaining your boundaries.

5. Maintain your boundaries confidently and assertively without guilt, apologies, or making excuses. Stand your ground like a tree in a hurricane—firm but not unkind.

6. You could check in with the person to find out if the solutions, options, or the people you suggested they approach could assist them. Also, you can check in to determine whether the compromise you offered them was valuable. If they encountered problems, you could look for ways to support them moving forward if you want to do that. Remember, you are not obligated to help someone if you do not want to.

Saying "No" in Personal Relationships

As a woman, I had difficulty saying "no" in personal relationships. I feared I would cause others' disapproval or shake things up in an important relationship.

I wish that, in the short term, I felt comfortable seeing the negative reactions due to my polite refusals. I also wish that, in the long term, I knew that saying "no" would strengthen the bond in my personal relationships and empower me. Here are practical tips on saying "no" in personal relationships to strengthen them and empower yourself:

- If you do not feel confident about saying "yes" or "no" to something, it is wise to take a moment before responding. Trust your intuition and allow yourself the time and space to think it over. It is okay to hit the pause button on a dramatic TV show—sometimes, you need a moment to process your thoughts. Remember, it is your right to take your time.

- Consider the long-term impact of saying "no" and if it aligns with your values. It is okay to feel uneasy about refusing something; it is a natural part of asserting your boundaries. It is like trying on a new pair of shoes—sometimes, you must walk around to see if they fit.

- When you feel ready to say "no," frame it around your priorities instead of pointing fingers. For example, instead of saying, "You are overpowering me and forcing my hand," it is better to say, "I cannot add anything else to my timetable right now." Using this approach will help you avoid confrontation and keep the conversation constructive. Remember, it is not a blame game—it is just you setting your boundaries.

- Accept the other person's reaction to your refusal. You are not responsible for them feeling a certain way. Acknowledge their feelings or reactions to your refusal but remain firm in your decision. For example, "I understand this might be disappointing, but I must prioritize my workload." It is like saying, "I get it; you are disappointed, but my plate's already full." This way, you show empathy without compromising your boundaries.

- Avoid providing many reasons or getting into debates that will not lead to a resolution. Being straightforward and brief is often more effective. Think of it as a mic drop—short, sweet, and to the point.

- Be gentle with yourself as you practice new habits. Change takes time, and setbacks are part of the journey. If you experience setbacks, implement your relapse prevention plan to get back on track again. Think of it as learning to ride a bike—wobbles and falls are part of the process, and if you fall off a bike, get back on it and try again. Mastering a new skill takes persistence.

- Consistency is crucial. When you assert your boundaries, you reinforce your self-worth and build self-confidence. It is like strengthening a core muscle—the more you exercise it, the stronger it becomes. So, keep at it, and celebrate your progress!

Interactive Element

Reflecting on your journey to overcome people-pleasing habits can be incredibly insightful. Use these guided journal prompts to explore your feelings and experiences of saying "no" respectfully and effectively.

- Describe your emotions when you first said "no" without further explanation.

  o How did it feel to assert your needs?

- o What thoughts ran through your mind?

- What surprised you the most about adjusting nonverbal cues to communicate assertiveness or empathy?

  - o Did you notice any changes in how others responded to you?

  - o How did these adjustments impact your confidence?

- Recall a recent situation where you set a clear boundary.

  - o What was the situation, and how did you handle it?

  - o How did the other person react, and how did you feel afterward?

- Consider a time when you struggled to say "no."

  - o What made it difficult?

  - o How did you eventually handle the situation?

- Think about the long-term benefits of setting boundaries.

  - o How has it impacted your relationships?

  - o What changes have you noticed in your overall well-being?

- Describe a situation where someone respected your boundary.

  - o How did it make you feel?

○ What did you learn from this experience?

These prompts help you delve deeper into your experiences and reinforce the importance of setting boundaries.

In the next chapter, you will learn about grounding techniques to manage your anxiety. I will discuss the normal reactions you can expect from others when asserting your boundaries. You will get to know signs of emotional manipulation. I will also discuss the philosophical concept of impermanence in relationships. I will elaborate on why accepting impermanence can help people make room for new connections and experiences.

You will also learn how to build a support system by identifying trustworthy people. Reciprocity is crucial in maintaining a support network. I will teach you how to cultivate it in your relationships using simple ways to show appreciation toward people who uplift you.

You will learn the difference between compassion, self-compassion, and self-validation. These three concepts enhanced my mental well-being along my journey. There are benefits to practicing self-validation alongside being compassionate toward yourself and showing compassion to others. I will provide details on how you can practice self-compassion by utilizing exercises that can help you boost your self-compassion.

Chapter Eight
Dealing With the Fallout

Have you ever faced a challenge that made your life much better after overcoming it yet left you feeling awkward, remorseful, anxious, or a combination of these emotions? That is what establishing a boundary feels like every time. I challenge you to manage these challenging emotions and others' reactions to establishing new boundaries, to let go and move forward when relationships need to change, to build a supportive community, and to practice self-compassion.

Handling Guilt and Anxiety After Saying "No"

Change is like trying to teach a cat to fetch—it is not always easy, and sometimes it feels like you are getting nowhere. Feeling guilty and anxious after asserting boundaries is perfectly normal. There are grounding techniques you can use to manage your anxiety. Grounding techniques are strategies intended to help people be in the moment and engage with what is happening in the present (BetterHelp Editorial Team, 2024). These are two types of grounding techniques: Mental grounding techniques involve activities that help you concentrate better, shift your mindset to take your power back, and promote relaxation. Physical grounding techniques include activities that use your body and the five senses to focus on positive thoughts. It aims to relax your nervous system to help your body return to its baseline and calm your mind.

Here are grounding techniques you can use to handle your anxiety after saying "no":

- **5-4-3-2-1 method:** It entails identifying five different things you can see, four textures you can touch, three sounds you can hear, two scents you can smell, and one thing you can taste.

- **Box breathing:** Take deep breaths slowly for four counts through your nose. Hold your breath for four counts. Relax your body during this pause. Exhale through your mouth for four counts. Lastly, hold your breath for four counts before you take another deep breath.

- **Mindfulness meditation:** You can listen to apps such as Headspace and Calm, along with guided meditation and mindfulness tools. Engaging in regular mindfulness meditation can help with decreasing anxiety levels, regaining control over your emotions, and boosting mental well-being.

- **Mindfulness:** Mindfulness is a valuable skill that helps people to remain grounded and non-judgmental in the here and now. You can teach yourself to be mindful or rely on meditation, yoga, and a type of therapy known as Mindfulness-Based Stress Reduction.

- **Exercise:** Regular physical activity releases those feel-good hormones known as endorphins that can boost your mood and reduce cortisol levels (i.e., stress hormones). Research has shown that exercise is significantly effective at reducing anxiety levels (Goodarzi et al., 2024; Teuber et al., 2024).

- **Progressive muscle relaxation:** Find a silent and comfortable spot to sit or lie on your back. Start by taking deep breaths, then begin tensing one muscle group at a time for five seconds. Relax each muscle group for 30 seconds. Repeat this process for every muscle group from your head to your toes.

- **Listen to music:** Listening to music can be a powerful tool to ground yourself when you feel anxious, as research has found that it can affect blood pressure, heart rate, and stress levels. To calm yourself, you can listen to relaxing or soothing music, solfeggio frequencies, or binaural beats.

- **Play games and puzzles:** Mental grounding tools such as crosswords, digital games and apps, and brain teasers take your mind away from anxious thoughts and keep your mind engaged in a pleasant distraction.

- **Spend time outdoors:** Being out in nature, smelling the flowers in your garden, getting sun exposure, going to different places, exploring your city or town, and simply spending time out of your house can help reduce anxiety.

- **Count backward:** Imagine counting from 100 in intervals of 8 (for example, 100, 92, 84, 76, 68 and continue until you reach 4 because that is the last number of this sequence). It is beneficial because counting backward forces your mind to mathematically work through a sequence in a structured way, which serves as a great distraction from anxious thoughts.

Navigating Others' Reactions to Your New Boundaries

When setting new boundaries with people who have always known you to say "yes," you can expect them not to understand why you are changing. They might argue with you and undermine your new boundaries in the worst-case scenario. If this happens, you might feel the urge to make people "get it," which can lead to frustration, stress, and, ultimately, the temptation to give up. But do not worry, this is not something you should experience, nor is it where you would want to be.

Take control of the matter, and remind yourself of the underlying intentions of setting your new boundaries. It is all about taking care of yourself. The resistance, frustration, confusion, guilt-tripping, or pushback you receive from others can be self-centered if they perceive your new boundaries as taking something away from them. Essentially, they are no longer getting what they want or believe they need from you, which can lead to criticisms.

When people criticize you for changing, remind yourself that their criticisms are not about you. It reveals their intention to get their way with you because it has worked in their favor for a long time. Remember, stay firm because it is not your responsibility to make them "get it."

When people want to regain power, control, benefits, superiority over you, favors, or privileges at your expense, it is essential to know the difference between healthy social influence and emotional manipulation (Ni, 2015). Healthy social influence is common in relationships that maintain reciprocity. When someone is emotionally manipulative, the relationship has an imbalance of power, and the manipulator is taking advantage of the other person for their agenda.

Here are some signs of emotional manipulation to help you recognize them:

- A manipulative person will want to meet and interact in a physical space in which they have control to exert dominance. This physical space is often somewhere you do not own or are familiar with.

- They will try to understand how you think and behave and look for strengths and weaknesses because they have a hidden agenda.

- They will manipulate facts to suit their agenda. Examples include lying, making excuses, distorting the truth, blaming you (the victim) for causing yourself to be taken advantage of, being two-faced, exaggerating, and considering only their opinion.

- Some people can use their hierarchical position in society, at work, or within family or friendship groups to maintain their status and power. At the same time, they can intentionally make your life harder. They can delay you from seeking the truth, hide mistakes, imperfections, and weaknesses, and avoid being scrutinized.

- When a manipulative person intentionally does not respond to your attempts to contact them, they believe they have power by delaying communication and playing mind games. They can use this silent treatment as leverage to get what they want.

- The manipulator can use the "playing dumb" strategy to pretend not to be aware of what you want them to do. They will let you take on their responsibility and stress yourself while fulfilling their duties. They can also "play dumb" to avoid responsibility or keep you in the dark.

Remember, maintaining your boundaries is crucial, especially when dealing with emotional manipulation. And if all else fails, imagine you are a cat—firm, independent, and not afraid to say "no" with a flick of your tail!

When Relationships Change: Letting Go and Moving Forward

The philosophical concept of impermanence comes from Eastern philosophies, especially Buddhism. Impermanence refers to the ever-changing nature of life (Nash, 2016). We often want to cling to people, possessions, relationships, jobs, accolades, income, and housing despite the reality that nothing lasts forever.

It is like trying to keep a snowman from melting in the summer when we cling to uncertain and temporary circumstances because we hope they will become permanent. It only worsens the pain and suffering when loss, grief, divorce, breakups, rejection, criticism, disappointment, and other trials come knocking on your doorstep with change.

Recognizing that impermanence exists in everything can trigger anxiety and stress about the nature of uncertainty and unpredictability of every aspect of life. However, it is essential to remember that nothing is permanent—even during times of pain, difficulty, suffering, and other trials. Understanding that these experiences, too, shall pass and change is like having a cosmic get-out-of-jail-free card, providing relief and reassurance.

In the context of relationships, embracing impermanence can lead to healthier and more fulfilling connections. Understanding that people and circumstances continuously evolve can help you manage expectations and embrace change. Accepting impermanence in relationships will make you resilient and adaptable to anything that happens. Additionally, recognizing that relationships are temporary means you will not have unrealistic expectations or become codependent on the other person. It does not mean you love or care less for the person; instead, it helps you live in the moment and appreciate your time with them. It encourages you to cherish moments and regularly express gratitude.

Accepting impermanence will teach you to navigate the ups and downs of relationships with maturity, wisdom, grace, and emotional intelligence. You will learn to let go and move forward when necessary, which will help you develop emotionally. Additionally, accepting impermanence opens you up to making room for new connections and experiences without being held back by past attachments, offering freedom and liberation.

So, the next time you reflect on the loss of friends, family, or partners after asserting your boundaries, remember: You can transform the pain of that loss into valuable lessons and personal growth. And who knows? You may find a new favorite pizza place along the way.

Building a Support System

Building a strong support system is essential for personal growth and resilience. You can follow these tips to assemble your team of trustworthy allies:

- Look for consistency in their actions and words: "Are they a man or woman of their word?" "Do they follow through on their promises and commitments?" Trustworthy people will always show up when they say they will and fulfill their commitments. If they say they will help you move, they will not suddenly develop a mysterious backache on a moving day.

- Pay attention to how they treat people from whom they have nothing to gain, such as waiters, waitresses, or people experiencing homelessness. People who are kind and respectful to those they have no vested interest in are likely to be honorable. Additionally, they are likely to be reliable if they treat people going through tough times with kindness, grace, respect, and support. If they tip well and say "please" and "thank you," you have a winner.

- Trustworthy people often listen actively and empathetically. They never listen to react; they listen to respond with insight and wisdom-giving. They make you feel heard and understood without judgment. They are a keeper if they remember your cat's name and favorite ice cream flavor.

- If you want to assess whether someone is trustworthy, evaluate their integrity. Reliable people have strong moral and ethical principles, character, and values. They are honest, firm, and successful, and they value fairness, equity, respect, and human dignity, even when it's difficult. Rest assured; they will also respect your boundaries. They will not ghost you when things get complicated.

Reciprocity is a mutual exchange of your needs and wants within relationships by contributing and receiving equally (Blackbyrn, 2024). When you consistently demonstrate support, love, compassion, and generosity, it shows that you are committed to the relationship. For example, when your sibling goes through a tough time. You offer support, advice, and a shoulder to cry on. In return, when you face challenges, they ensure they are there for you, providing the same level of support and understanding. Mutual support, respect, trust, and understanding strengthen your bond and make you feel loved, valued, and appreciated. It creates a positive, harmonious, constructive, and balanced relationship. You can cultivate reciprocity by showing genuine interest in each other's lives, doing small acts of kindness, sharing your thoughts, feelings, and responsibilities honestly, and regularly expressing gratitude with a simple "thank you." These can all reinforce positive behavior and encourage reciprocity.

Besides saying a heartfelt "thank you" to someone to show appreciation, here are simple ways to show appreciation toward people who uplift you:

- A handwritten note can be a cherished token of appreciation for the valuable time you took to write a thoughtful message on how much you appreciate them. Also, it is a great way to show off your fancy stationery.

- Small gestures or gifts can show that you care, appreciate their support, and are thinking of them. Some people appreciate little gestures or actions rather than gifts; as the saying goes, actions speak louder than words. Small gestures can include offering to pay for or help them with something, inviting them to social events, or making them laugh.

- Showing up for someone can make them feel valued and appreciated. Showing up for someone can mean different things, such as being on time for whatever they may be doing or needing you for, keeping promises, and doing what you said you would do.

- Spend quality time together. Consider dedicating time to doing something the other person enjoys doing. Shared experiences can strengthen your bond.

- Offer to help them with tasks or challenges they might be facing. It is a huge help and shows that you are there for them, just as they are for you, making it a great way to show them how you feel.

❧

Self-Compassion Practices for the Recovering People-Pleaser

Do you know the difference between compassion and self-compassion? Compassion involves putting yourself in another person's shoes to feel and understand their suffering. Recognizing their suffering can lead to doing what you can to alleviate it. The elements of compassion include empathy, kindness, and a desire to help. Imagine seeing someone in a low mood and approaching them with a soft gaze and a gentle tone, saying, "Hi, I noticed you are feeling down. Want to talk about it?"

On the other hand, self-compassion involves offering yourself the same kindness, understanding, and assistance you offer others. It means treating yourself with the same care and concern you would show a friend or family member going through a tough time. The elements of self-compassion include self-kindness, raised consciousness, and self-awareness. Imagine you make a financial mistake that lowers your credit score. Instead of being self-critical, you channel your inner superhero and say, "It is understandable that I am disappointed. Everyone makes mistakes. I will learn from this and do better next time. For now, I will take deep breaths and remind myself that I am capable and doing my best."

Self-validation is like being your own best friend. It involves acknowledging and accepting that your feelings, thoughts, and experiences are valid and important. It helps you recognize your emotions without judgment and understand that they are a natural part of life. Practicing self-validation alongside self-compassion can lead to several benefits, including building your self-worth, reducing the need for external validation, learning to manage your emotions more effectively, and fostering a positive self-view, which can reduce feelings of anxiety and depression, significantly enhancing your emotional well-being and confidence (Guthrie, 2023; Martin, 2019; Sockolov, 2024).

Here are ways you can practice and enhance self-compassion to help you get started:

- Take a minute to acknowledge your emotions whenever you feel stressed, frustrated, or angry. You can say this to yourself: "This is probably the most difficult time of my life right now. However, you know what? I will get through this. Everything I have gone through has prepared me for this moment."

- Spend some time writing about the tough time you are experiencing. Reflect on your feelings and what you should do to handle the situation. Write this passage in a manner that expresses compassion, support, and understanding.

- If you are self-critical, reframe those destructive thoughts into compassionate and constructive ones. For example, instead of saying, "I am so stupid for not seeing that it was too good to be true," try saying, "At least I know better now. It is okay to be bamboozled once."

- Imagine having a conversation with your younger self. Speak to yourself with kindness, reassurance, and compassion as you would with a child in need. It is a beautiful exercise that can facilitate a connection with your inner child and heal past wounds.

Interactive Element

Here is a checklist to help you as a recovering people-pleaser navigate the aftermath of setting boundaries, including strategies for managing anxiety and practicing self-compassion and self-validation:

- Use grounding techniques such as the 5-4-3-2-1 method, box breathing, mindfulness meditation, mindfulness in daily interactions, exercise, progressive muscle relaxation, listening to soft or relaxing music, playing games and puzzles, spending time outdoors, and counting backward to manage anxiety after asserting your boundaries.

- Make self-compassion a part of your daily routine. Start your day by checking in with yourself, acknowledging your feelings, and identifying your needs. Throughout the day, take moments to offer yourself kindness. In the evening, reflect on your efforts, progress, and things you are grateful for in a diary or journal entry.

- To incorporate self-validation into your daily routine, you could reframe negative thoughts into compassionate ones whenever you catch yourself being self-critical.

- You can use self-validation statements as daily affirmations to validate your worth and feelings. For example, "It is okay to feel this way," "I am worthy of love and respect," "I am doing my best," and "My needs are valid."

Remember, setting and asserting boundaries and practicing self-compassion and self-validation are ongoing processes. Be patient with yourself and celebrate your wins along the way.

In the next chapter, I will conclude by reiterating the transformative power of the book's central message, inspiring you to embrace change and growth. Additionally, I will provide a summary of the main points of each chapter. I will reflect on the value of overcoming people-pleasing habits and the resilience, perseverance, dedication, and growth developed through navigating challenges and learning to embrace your self-worth.

Conclusion

The book's central message is to embrace change and growth and achieve self-preservation by learning to put yourself first. You have learned to do this by setting healthy boundaries and staying firm to uphold your self-respect, power, self-worth, self-care, emotional integrity, and overall well-being.

People-pleasing is a learned behavior that can be overcome. It often stems from underlying motivations such as fear of rejection, abandonment, low self-esteem and self-worth, and the need for external validation. Behavioral patterns rooted in codependency and a desire to be seen as perfect also contribute to these people-pleasing behaviors. Signs and symptoms of people-pleasing arise from childhood experiences, societal expectations, and cultural influences.

Children raised by parents with BPD who have difficulty regulating their emotions can cause these children to internalize feelings of worthlessness and shame. These children often learn to put other's needs first to seek approval and avoid conflict. In collectivist cultures, children are socialized to maintain a harmonious, positive environment at all costs, making asserting their needs in adulthood challenging. Conversely, children are encouraged to advocate for themselves assertively and confidently in individualistic cultures. Cultural influences, such as ethnicity, community values, and socially desirable behavior, significantly shape people-pleasing behaviors in adulthood.

Constantly saying "yes" to others can lead to stress and anxiety, driven by a fear of rejection, criticism, failure, or conflict. It can result in unhealthy coping mechanisms and resentment as your needs go unmet.

People-pleasing can cause burnout, with physical symptoms like chronic fatigue, sleep problems, gastrointestinal issues, headaches, heartburn, increased risk of substance abuse, overeating, heart disease, hypertension, muscle pain, and a weakened immune system. Emotional symptoms can include concentration problems, depressed mood, low self-esteem, cynicism, and mood swings. Behavioral symptoms are often social withdrawal and decreased work performance, motivation, or job satisfaction.

Triggers for burnout in people-pleasers include feeling not in control, the urge to say "yes," overcommitment, lack of boundaries, the need for external validation, and a fear of conflict. While valuing relationships and prioritizing others is important, balancing this with self-care is crucial. Overcommitment and underappreciation can lead to a "siege mentality" and a lack of self-advocacy. Financially, people-pleasing can result in poor decisions that affect long-term stability.

Making intentional choices benefits your well-being by helping you understand your needs, values, and desires. Setting boundaries protects your emotional and mental health, time, resources, and energy. Saying "yes" to yourself helps you prioritize self-care, overcome negative thinking, build a support system, and embrace mistakes as growth opportunities.

Self-reflection helps identify your actual needs and desires in various situations. Aligning actions with values involves identifying personal values, principles, and beliefs that influence behavior. Misalignment is normal, but accountability systems can help realign actions with values.

Trusting yourself and listening to your inner wisdom leads to better choices than letting fear or anxiety influence your decisions. Self-awareness is key for providing clarity and helping identify intuitive signals.

A personal mission statement guides decision-making and helps you to achieve long-term goals by envisioning who you want to be and what you want to accomplish. Benefits include better self-understanding, accountability to long-term objectives, setting and communicating boundaries, and shifting focus from people-pleasing to internal fulfillment.

To break free from people-pleasing, start small. Say "no" to small requests by acknowledging them, expressing appreciation, giving a simple explanation for refusing, offering alternatives, and embracing self-validation.

Building confidence in your decision-making entails gathering your thoughts, ensuring decisions align with your vision, avoiding seeking too many opinions, listening to your intuition, listing pros and cons, focusing on growth opportunities, and standing by your decisions.

Identify core values and priorities by self-reflecting, self-coaching, brainstorming a list of values, narrowing them down to 10-15, choosing your top five, arranging them by importance, and revisiting them as needed.

To improve time management: Establish boundaries, change behavior gradually, prioritize tasks aligned with your values, consider requests thoroughly, assess the impact of saying "yes," assertively say "no," ensure your relationships are reciprocal, and help when you genuinely want to.

To stay the course, prioritize self-care by setting boundaries, celebrating small wins, speaking positively to yourself, setting clear SMART goals, and treating yourself regularly.

Boundaries involve identifying your limits, assertively communicating them, and holding people accountable if they disrespect them. Maintaining boundaries is crucial for protecting your health, enriching relationships through effective communication, and enhancing life satisfaction. Boundaries also boost self-esteem, reduce stress, and help develop resilience.

Saying "no" is an act of self-care, not selfishness. It helps you be your best for yourself and others, making you more present and supportive. Saying "no" conserves your energy for what matters most.

Physical, emotional, time, and work boundaries help you feel at ease, protect your emotional needs, set realistic expectations, and balance work with life. Setting boundaries makes you aware of others' needs, enhances self-respect, fosters harmony, models healthy behavior, boosts self-esteem, and reduces stress and anxiety.

Common myths about boundaries include the boundary-maker being selfish, negative, rude, or that boundaries are harmful to relationships. In reality, boundaries are acts of self-care. They help people create healthy relationships, improve communication, and save you from tolerating nonsense.

Self-concept involves understanding yourself through social interactions, experiences, and self-reflection. To redefine it, examine your current self-concept, identify and challenge self-critical beliefs, replace them with positive ones, visualize your ideal self, and take consistent actions that align with this vision—challenge limiting beliefs with contradicting evidence, positive affirmations, and having supportive people.

Reclaim your agency by setting boundaries and saying "no" to regain control, empower yourself, assert your autonomy, shape your relationship dynamics, foster mutually respectful and beneficial relationships, and practice self-care and self-compassion. Use assertiveness techniques like "I" statements, a firm tone, active listening, the fogging technique, and staying resolute to stand your ground confidently.

Setbacks are normal. Reframe setbacks as learning opportunities, practice self-compassion, rely on a support network, stay flexible and adaptable, and create a relapse prevention plan to cope with setbacks. Celebrate progress to stay motivated by journaling wins, sharing the news with loved ones, making a small trophy, pampering yourself, and taking photos.

Setting boundaries impacts others positively by inspiring them to prioritize their needs and state and assert their boundaries.

Techniques for saying "no" gracefully and effectively are replacing "no" with "let me get back to you later," roleplaying to build confidence, using body language to support your "no," and using gentle gestures to convey warmth. The book includes over 20 scripts and phrases to help you say "no" in daily interactions.

Physical distance shows comfort level, intimacy, formality, or desire for personal space. Respectively, a soothing, sharp, or warm tone shows gracefulness, frustration, support, and empathy. A high pitch shows enthusiasm or surprise, while a low pitch shows seriousness or calmness. A loud voice conveys authority or urgency, and a soft voice creates intimacy or confidentiality.

Follow these practical tips for saying "no" in professional settings: State your boundaries early to set a precedent, frame refusals politely and show appreciation, provide context, propose alternatives, maintain your boundaries firmly, and follow up on suggestions.

Try these effective strategies to decline in personal situations gracefully: Trust your gut feeling and ask for time to think. Assess the implications of saying "no" and your comfort level. Make refusals about you, not others. Accept others' reactions without guilt. Avoid frivolous arguments and use a relapse prevention plan to get back on track if needed.

Grounding techniques involve mental and physical activities, such as the 5-4-3-2-1 method and backward counting. You can use both of these, amongst other grounding techniques, to manage anxiety after asserting boundaries.

You can expect resistance, frustration, confusion, guilt-tripping, or pushback from others when asserting boundaries. Beware of signs of emotional manipulation such as meeting and interacting with you in familiar spaces to the manipulator to exert dominance, using hidden agendas, twisting facts to suit their agenda, engaging in power plays, silent treatment, and "playing dumb."

Understanding the concept of impermanence in relationships helps you let go and move forward when necessary and makes room for new connections and experiences because nothing lasts forever.

Identifying trustworthy people to become your support system is crucial. Look for consistency in their actions and words. Notice their treatment of people they are not vested in, ability to listen actively and empathetically, and integrity. Reciprocity is an integral part of maintaining a good support network. Cultivate reciprocity to show appreciation with handwritten notes, give small gifts, be reliable, spend quality time, and offer help to people who uplift you.

Simply put, compassion is about being kind to others, self-compassion is about being kind to yourself, and self-validation is about accepting and acknowledging your emotions, thoughts, and experiences as valid and important. Practicing self-validation alongside self-compassion and compassion is highly beneficial for building your self-esteem, developing a positive self-view, managing your emotions, and reducing anxiety and depression. You can practice self-compassion by acknowledging your emotions, writing about tough times compassionately, reframing self-critical thoughts into compassionate ones, and nurturing your inner child.

Overcoming people-pleasing habits is rewarding for navigating challenges and learning to embrace self-worth with grace, firmness, dedication, resilience, and purpose.

I would love to hear your thoughts and views on this book and how it helped along your boundary-setting journey. Please leave a review on Amazon. It is greatly appreciated.

Bonus Content:
A Special Gift Just for You!

As a thank you for investing in your personal growth, I'm excited to offer you a Self-Love Journal for Women!

The Complete Self-Love Journal for Women

This guide is designed to support your journey of self-compassion and reflection. It includes:

✦ 365 prompts to inspire daily reflection
✦ Focus topics to nurture different aspects of your well-being

Remember, self-love is a continuous journey, and each step you take is a powerful act of self-compassion and growth. Let this journal guide you, support you, and remind you of the incredible strength and beauty that resides within you.

SCAN ME☐

H.L. Nakamura, RN-BSN
Author, Owner of Radiant Beauty RN

Glossary

- **Accountability:** An aspect of change that is central to improving one's life. Accountable people can hold themselves responsible for the desired change in their lives or rely on assistance from someone else.

- **Active listening:** An art of communication that involves listening attentively, nodding, paraphrasing, asking clarifying questions, being fully present in the conversation, paying attention to body language, and responding respectfully and effectively to show you understand what the speaker is saying.

- **Assert:** To confidently speak and effectively get your intentions across to someone, leading to better communication and understanding.

- **Assertiveness:** It is a skill for setting boundaries by confidently expressing your needs, desires, and thoughts and ensuring they are clearly understood while respecting others.

- **Authenticity:** Being true to who you are, what truly matters to you, and where you come from, living in alignment with your core beliefs, values, and identity.

- **Autonomy:** It is the freedom to make decisions and take actions independently without being swayed by external influences.

- **Borderline personality disorder:** A mental health condition characterized by emotional instability, erratic behavior, distorted self-image, and impaired functioning, which can lead to impulsivity and unhealthy relationships.

- **Boundaries:** Limits one sets on their own and communicates to another person concerning their specific situation, availability, and capacity without fear, compromise, or seeking approval to protect their well-being and ensure their needs are respected.

- **Boundary-setting:** Identifying and effectively communicating one's availability and capacity to assist others while being self-respecting, self-compassionate, and self-caring.

- **Burnout:** It is a form of exhaustion caused by prolonged and excessive stress, often resulting from working yourself too hard at the expense of your physical, emotional, and mental health.

- **Chronic anxiety:** It is a term used to describe a form of anxiety that persists for an extended period of time and may not be triggered by a specific situation, person, or event. It often manifests in continuous, excessive worry that can interfere with daily functioning.

- **Chronic depression:** A term used to describe a form of depression that persists for at least two years. It is typical for someone with chronic depression to present clinically with a continuous low mood and other symptoms that can interfere with daily functioning.

- **Chronic stress:** A prolonged and continuous state of physiological and psychological overwhelm that can negatively affect one's health if left untreated.

- **Codependency:** A condition where one heavily relies on someone else to gain approval or praise to feel secure in their decision-making, judgments, and abilities.

- **Compassion:** An emotional response that entails putting yourself in another person's shoes to empathize with and understand their suffering and then doing your best to help alleviate it.

- **Compromise:** A way for two people to meet one another halfway, where one person agrees to a concession from the other.

- **Congruence:** This occurs when your self-image and ideal self are closely aligned or overlap significantly.

- **Coping mechanism:** A strategy or technique to help manage stress, anxiety, or overwhelming situations in a healthy manner, either independently or with the support of a medical professional.

- **Criticism:** The act of expressing disapproval or providing constructive feedback about something or someone.

- **Cultural relativism:** A concept that encourages individuals to appreciate and respect the values, knowledge, and behaviors of diverse cultures without imposing one's cultural norms and judgments on others.

- **Dopamine:** A neurotransmitter responsible for the pleasure and rewards system in the brain. It helps regulate mood, motivation, and feelings of pleasure.

- **Effective communication:** The art of expressing your thoughts, feelings, desires, and needs clearly to another person while ensuring they understand.

- **Emotional boundaries:** Limits and rules that protect or preserve your thoughts, feelings, and emotional needs in relationships and interactions.

- **Emotional exhaustion:** A state of feeling emotionally depleted or drained due to prolonged stress from either professional or personal life, or sometimes both.

- **Emotional integrity:** Being honest with others about your feelings and emotional availability regarding a particular situation, person, or event.

- **Emotional manipulation:** It is a form of emotional abuse within relationships that have an imbalance of power, and the manipulator takes advantage of the other person for their agenda.

- **Existentialism:** It is a philosophical inquiry into human existence from its purpose, meaning, and value, and it stresses that people have personal freedom, responsibility, and free will to make choices that determine their development.

- **External Validation:** It is a tendency to constantly seek approval or praise from others to feel better about oneself.

- **Fear of abandonment:** The tendency to believe people will distance themselves from you, often based on irrational thoughts and anxieties.

- **Fear of rejection or disapproval:** The tendency to believe that people dislike or disapprove of you, often based on false perceptions and irrational thoughts.

- **Financial boundaries:** Limits one sets on the financial assistance one can afford to provide others while ensuring one's financial stability and independence.

- **Gracefulness:** A subtle art of communication that conveys gentleness in the delivery, tone, and intention behind our words and actions.

- **Grounding techniques:** These are strategies intended to help people be in the moment and engage with what is happening in the present.

- **Incongruence:** This happens when your self-image and ideal self are significantly different.

- **Ideal self:** The idea or mental image of who you want to be.

- **Impermanence:** A philosophical concept that refers to accepting that nothing lasts forever and is promised in every aspect of life.

- **Intuition:** A gut feeling that pulls you toward a specific decision or choice that seems to be in your best interest or a sudden insight you receive.

- **Insecure:** When a person does not feel confident about themselves or an aspect of themself.

- **Insecurity:** When someone lacks confidence, which can affect various aspects of their life.

- **Insomnia:** A sleep disorder that is characterized by trouble with falling or staying asleep, often resulting in the need to seek medical assistance to treat.

- **Job satisfaction:** Feeling fulfilled with your job to the extent that you love and look forward to going to work every day.

- **Mental grounding techniques:** These activities help you focus, regain control, and relax.

- **Mindfulness:** A state of being present in the moment, being aware of your surroundings, thoughts, and actions, and maintaining a sense of calm about what is happening around you.

- **Mutual respect:** It is a common understanding between two parties that their needs and boundaries are equally important and should be honored in the relationship.

- **Narcissistic personality disorder:** A mental health condition characterized by an inflated sense of self-importance and superiority, an excessive need for attention and admiration, and a lack of empathy.

- **Operant conditioning:** A learning process that involves reinforcement and punishment to increase or decrease the likelihood of a behavior.

- **Overcommitment:** The tendency to take on more tasks or an increased workload that one can handle comfortably.

- **People-pleasing:** A behavior where one puts someone else's needs and desires first over their own, often at the expense of their well-being.

- **People-pleasing cycle:** It is a pattern of behavior where one prioritizes others' needs and desires at the expense of their own.

- **People-pleasing habits:** Behaviors centered around meeting the expectations of other people, often at the expense of one's own needs and desires.

- **Perfectionism:** A tendency to strive to meet high standards that are often impossible to achieve.

- **Personality disorder:** A mental health condition where inflexible and pervasive patterns of behavior, cognition, and inner experience deviate significantly from one's cultural norms, leading to distress or impairment in various areas of functioning.

- **Personal mission statement:** A concise statement that defines your values, goals, and purpose to help you navigate life's decisions and stay committed to becoming who you want to be and what you want to accomplish.

- **Physical boundaries:** Limits and rules that protect or preserve your personal space, physical comfort with touch, and individual privacy.

- **Physical grounding techniques:** These activities help your body and the five senses to focus on positive thoughts by relaxing your nervous system to help your body return to its baseline and calm your mind.

- **Positive reinforcement:** The learning process of increasing the likelihood of a desired behavior by adding a pleasant stimulus.

- **Proxemics:** The physical distance between yourself and others and how this influences interactions and relationships.

- **Reciprocity:** Equal give and take in relationships.

- **Reinforcement:** A technique from behavioral psychology used to increase the likelihood of a behavior by using a stimulus. It is part of the broader framework of operant conditioning.

- **Resentment:** Bitterness or anger when someone feels the other person has treated them unfairly or wrongly, especially in a relationship.

- **Respect:** A positive feeling of valuing your own needs, desires, boundaries, and well-being as much as you value those of others, acknowledging that both are deserving of consideration.

- **Self-actualization:** Reaching your full potential.

- **Self-affirmation:** A statement that acknowledges and reinforces your inherent worth and value, often focusing on your strengths, abilities, and positive qualities.

- **Self-awareness:** Recognizing and understanding your thoughts, emotions, and behaviors without judgment.

- **Self-care:** A beneficial practice involving activities to nurture your physical, emotional, and mental well-being, leading to a healthier and more balanced life.

- **Self-coaching:** A process of using your identity, values, beliefs, thoughts, and past experiences to guide your growth and development.

- **Self-compassion:** Extending warmth and understanding toward oneself in times of feeling inadequate, experiencing failure, or enduring general suffering.

- **Self-concept:** The knowledge of who we are physically, socially, and personally, as well as our beliefs, attributes, behaviors, and abilities.

- **Self-confidence:** An empowering attitude that encourages belief in and acceptance of oneself while recognizing one's skills, abilities, strengths, and weaknesses and feeling in control of one's life.

- **Self-critical:** A negative tendency to be harsh on yourself for making common mistakes in life.

- **Self-esteem:** Confidence in one's worth, abilities, skills, and morals. In terms of self-concept, self-esteem refers to your overall evaluation about yourself including strengths and weaknesses.

- **Self-image:** Your knowledge about yourself, including your physicality, social roles, and unique traits.

- **Selfishness:** Thinking and caring only about your needs and desires, disregarding others.

- **Self-perception:** The way you view yourself, including your thoughts, feelings, and behaviors.

- **Self-preservation:** The act of protecting oneself from physical, emotional, and mental suffering caused by one's environment, situations, and the people around them.

- **Self-reflection:** Giving serious thought to any matter in one's life.

- **Self-respect:** Recognizing your worth and knowing when to leave or stand up for yourself in situations or places where people do not treat you with the kindness and care you deserve.

- **Self-sacrifice:** The act of giving up one's interests, desires, and goals for the benefit of others.

- **Self-validation:** Recognizing and accepting your feelings, thoughts, needs, and desires as valid, without judgment.

- **Self-worth:** Recognizing and acknowledging that you are a person of value.

- **Social conditioning:** The sociological process of shaping people's behavior, beliefs, and desires through interactions and the cultural norms in a society.

- **Socialization:** The lifelong process of learning and internalizing norms, values, and behaviors that are socially acceptable in a society, starting from childhood and continuing through interactions with family, peers, friends, schools, and media.

- **Symbolic interactionism:** It is a sociological theory that focuses on how people use language and symbols to communicate and the importance of social interactions in shaping our perceptions and meanings.

- **The fogging technique:** It is a communication strategy that involves acknowledging the other person's emotions without escalating the conflict, often by expressing understanding while remaining calm and composed.

- **Therapy:** Treatment for mental conditions through verbal communication and interaction led by a trained mental health professional.

- **Time boundaries:** Limits and rules set to manage one's time commitments and protect them from over-commitment. Being intentional with your time can help you set aside time for different aspects of life, such as spending quality time with family and friends, treating yourself, meditating for an hour, and more.

- **Underappreciation:** Situations where others do not recognize or take your efforts for granted.

- **Values:** Principles that are significant in one's life that guide behavior, decisions, and judgments.

- **Work-life balance:** Allocating time to work and various activities that make up one's life, such as catching up with family and friends.

References

Ackerman, C. E. (2018, June 07). *What is self-concept theory? A psychologist explains.* PositivePsychology.com. https://positivepsychology.com/self-concept/

Ackerman, C. E. (2017, December 21). *8 powerful self-compassion exercises & worksheets (+ pdf).* PositivePsychology.com. https://positivepsychology.com/self-compassion-exercises-worksheets/

Amabile, T. M., & Kramer, S. J. (2011, May). *The power of small wins.* Harvard Business Review. https://hbr.org/2011/05/the-power-of-small-wins

Attard, A. (2022, November 28). *The meaning and different movements of compassion.* Psychology Today. https://www.psychologytoday.com/us/blog/human-beings-being-human/202211/the-meaning-and-different-movements-compassion?msockid=294f886df6906a60268d9b69f7906bc7

Attard, A. (2021, May 06). *Accepting impermanence can help us live more flexibly.* Psychology Today. https://www.psychologytoday.com/us/blog/human-beings-being-human/202105/accepting-impermanence-can-help-us-live-more-flexibly

Ball, S. (n.d.). *Breaking free: Unravelling the roots of people-pleasing and codependency.* Codependency Recovery. https://codependencyrecovery.org/2024/04/06/breaking-free-unravelling-the-roots-of-people-pleasing-and-codependency/

Barreca, G. (2020, March 25). *Fear of disappointing others: How to cope and what to learn.* Psychology Today. https://www.psychologytoday.com/us/blog/snow-white-doesnt-live-here-anymore/202003/fear-disappointing-others-how-cope-and-what-learn

Bastos, F. (2024, March 04). *The psychology of being a people pleaser: Understanding, signs, risks, and how to stop.* MindOwl. https://mindowl.org/being-a-people-pleaser/

Bennett, T. (n.d.). *People-pleasing: A breakdown of the bad habit and how to kick it.* Thriveworks. https://thriveworks.com/help-with/self-improvement/people-pleasing/

Berzin, A. (n.d.). *Impermanence as a resource for healthy relationships.* Study Buddhism. https://studybuddhism.com/en/tibetan-buddhism/mind-training/handling-the-challenges-of-life/impermanence-as-a-resource-for-healthy-relationships

BetterHelp Editorial Team. (2024, June 13). *10 best grounding techniques for anxiety related disorders.* BetterHelp. https://www.betterhelp.com/advice/anxiety/22-best-grounding-techniques-for-anxiety/

Birenbaum, B. (n.d.). *Assertiveness: Definition, examples, & techniques.* The Berkeley Well-Being Institute. https://www.berkeleywellbeing.com/assertiveness.html

Blackbyrn, S. (2024, February 10). *What is reciprocity in relationships?* Coach Foundation.

https://coachfoundation.com/blog/what-is-reciprocity-in-relationships/

Boundaries. (n.d.). Psychology Today. https://www.psychologytoday.com/us/basics/boundaries?msockid=294f886df6906a60268d9b69f7906bc7

Buggy, P. (n.d.). *5 steps to define your core values: A compass for navigating life's decisions.* Mindful Ambition. https://mindfulambition.net/values/

Burnout. (n.d.). Psychology Today. https://www.psychologytoday.com/us/basics/burnout?msockid=294f886df6906a60268d9b69f7906bc7

Chain, J. (2024, February 16). *Signs you are a people-pleaser and how to stop.* Thrive for the People. https://www.thriveforthepeople.com/blog/signs-you-are-a-people-pleaser-and-how-to-stop

Cherry, K. (2024a, May 19). *How to stop people-pleasing.* Verywell Mind. https://www.verywellmind.com/how-to-stop-being-a-people-pleaser-5184412

Cherry, K. (2024b, July 29). *What is self-concept?* Verywell Mind. https://www.verywellmind.com/what-is-self-concept-2795865

Cherry, K. (2022, October 06). *10 ways to build resilience.* Verywell Mind. https://www.verywellmind.com/ways-to-become-more-resilient-2795063

Cikanavicius, D. (2017, August 28). *The trap of external validation for self-esteem.* PsychCentral. https://psychcentral.com/blog/psychology-self/2017/08/validation-self-esteem#1

Cohen, I. S. (2024, January 22). *Breaking the cycle of people-pleasing.* Psychology Today. https://www.psychologytoday.com/us/blog/your-emotional-meter/202401/breaking-the-cycle-of-people-pleasing

Coping with relapse: Strategies for resilience and progress in addiction recovery. (n.d.). AM Health Care. https://amhealthcare.org/coping-with-relapse-strategies-for-resilience/

Copley, L. (2024, May 24). *How to say no & master the art of personal freedom.* PositivePsychology.com. https://positivepsychology.com/how-to-say-no/#why-you-should-learn-to-say-no

Creating a personal mission statement: Inspiring examples. (n.d.). Resumehead. https://resumehead.com/blog/personal-mission-statement

Cross, R., Dillion, K., & Greenberg, D. (2021, January 29). *The secret to building resilience.* Harvard Business Review. https://hbr.org/2021/01/the-secret-to-building-resilience

Degges-White, S. (2023, September 19). *10 ways that better boundaries can improve your life.* Psychology Today. https://www.psychologytoday.com/intl/blog/lifetime-connections/202111/10-ways-that-better-boundaries-can-improve-your-life?msockid=294f886df6906a60268d9b69f7906bc7

di Giacomo, E., Andreini, E., Lorusso, O., & Clerici, M. (2023). The dark side of empathy in narcissistic personality disorder. *Frontiers in Psychiatry, 14,* 1074558.

8 dimensions of wellness. (n.d.). University of Southern Indiana. https://www.usi.edu/hr/benefits/8-dimensions-of-wellness

11 ways to stop feeling overly responsible for others. (n.d.). Awake Mindful. https://awakemindful.com/stop-feeling-responsible-for-others/

Embracing the impermanence of life for inner peace and purpose. (n.d.). Transitions and Beginnings. https://transitionsandbeginnings.com/embracing-the-impermanence-of-life-for-inner-peace-and-purpose/

Existentialism is a humanism. (2024, June 08). Wikipedia. https://en.wikipedia.org/wiki/Existentialism_Is_a_Humanism

Feinstein, S. (n.d.). *Fear of disappointing others and what you can do to conquer it.* Advanced Behavioral Health. https://behaviortherapynyc.com/fear-of-disappointing-others-and-what-you-can-do-to-conquer-it/

15 types of healthy boundaries and how to communicate them. (n.d.). Center for Mindful Psychotherapy. https://mindfulcenter.org/15-types-of-healthy-boundaries-and-how-to-communicate-them/

57 special ideas on how to pamper yourself today: A woman's guide to self-care. (2023, September 06). The Pocket Diary. https://www.thepocketdiary.com/57-special-ideas-on-how-to-pamper-yourself-today-a-womans-guide-to-self-care/

Fitzgerald, C. (2023, August 20). *Saying no professionally: Essential workplace skill.* Oak Innovation.

https://www.oakinnovation.com/blog/free-business-skills/saying-no-professionally

5 ways to respond to people who violate your boundaries. (2023, May 21). Power of Positivity. https://www.powerofpositivity.com/5-ways-to-respond-to-people-who-violate-your-boundaries/

eNotAlone. (2023, March 04). *Seven key indicators to help you identify trustworthy people.* https://www.enotalone.com/article/relationships/seven-key-indicators-to-help-you-identify-trustworthy-people-r2647/

Fleming, L. (2024, March 28). *When should you trust your intuition?* Verywell Mind. https://www.verywellmind.com/when-to-trust-your-intuition-7481322

Forsey, C. (2021, January 25). *Here's how to write an impressive personal mission statement [Examples & Template].* HubSpot. https://blog.hubspot.com/marketing/personal-mission-statement

Franzoni, M. (2023, July 23). *Taming the beast: Conquering your fear of disappointing others.* Zella Life. https://www.zellalife.com/blog/fear-of-disappointing-others/

Fritscher, L. (2024, July 01). *Understanding fear of abandonment.* Verywell Mind. https://www.verywellmind.com/fear-of-abandonment-2671741

Gelberg-Goff, L. M. (n.d.). *Dealing with the consequences: How to handle the reactions of others to your new boundaries.* Loren Gelberg-Goff. https://lorengelberggoff.com/dealing-with-the-consequences-how-to-handle-the-reactions-of-others-to-your-new-boundaries/

Geteffadmin. (2023, July 05). *Celebrating milestones: Why recognizing progress is important for long-term achievement.* DayViewer Blog. https://blog.dayviewer.com/celebrating-milestones-why-recognizing-progress-is-important-for-long-term-achievement/

Glaser, J. E. (2015, December 28). *Celebration time.* Psychology Today. https://www.psychologytoday.com/us/blog/conversational-intelligence/201512/celebration-time

Goodarzi, S., Teymouri Athar, M. M., Beiky, M., Fathi, H., Nakhaee, Z., Omran, S. P., & Shafiee, A. (2024). Effect of physical activity for reducing anxiety symptoms in older adults: A meta-analysis of randomized controlled trials. *BMC Sports Science, Medicine and Rehabilitation, 16*(1), 153. https://doi.org/10.1186/s13102-024-00947-w

Gupta, A. (2024, July 17). *No man is an island meaning, examples, synonyms.* Leverage Edu. https://leverageedu.com/explore/learn-english/no-man-is-an-island-idiom-meaning-with-example/#:~:text=The%20meaning%20of%20the%20English%20idiom%20%E2%80%9Cno%20man,people%20need%20support%2C%20companionship%2C%20and%20collaboration%20to%20thrive.

Guthrie, G. (2023, November 17). *Supercharge productivity with the power of self-validation*. Nulab. https://nulab.com/learn/collaboration/self-validation-will-boost-your-productivity/

Guttman, J. (2023, August 02). *Breaking the habit of people pleasing*. Psychology Today. https://www.psychologytoday.com/us/blog/sustainable-life-satisfaction/202308/breaking-the-habit-of-people-pleasing

Hadiah. (n.d.). *What is external validation? Top 5 ways to stop relying on it*. Ineffable Living. https://ineffableliving.com/what-is-external-validation/#:~:text=Moreover%2C%20people%20who%20rely%20heavily%20on%20external%20validation,from%20fully%20exploring%20their%20own%20identities%20and%20values.

Harris, L. (2021, December 10). *Six steps to identify and align your personal core values*. Forbes. https://www.forbes.com/councils/forbescoachescouncil/2020/09/21/six-steps-to-identify-and-align-your-personal-core-values/

Hendriksen, E. (2021, May 18). *5 ways to stop being a people pleaser*. Psychology Today. https://www.psychologytoday.com/ca/blog/how-to-be-yourself/202105/5-ways-to-stop-being-a-people-pleaser

Herrity, J. (2024, July 08). *How to write a personal mission statement (with examples)*. Indeed. https://www.indeed.com/career-advice/career-development/personal-mission-statement-examples

Hitchcock, S. (2024, March 11). *The journey to self-validation: Overcoming the need for external approval.* ClearVision Psychotherapy & Equine Assisted Therapy. https://www.clear-vision-psychotherapy.com/blog/the-journey-to-self-validation-overcoming-the-need-for-external-approval

Hopper, E. (2018, April 24). *Why being a perfectionist can be harmful.* ThoughtCo. https://www.thoughtco.com/understanding-perfectionism-4161254

How happy happens in your brain. (2015, May 17). The Best Brain Possible. https://thebestbrainpossible.com/how-happy-happens-in-your-brain/

How to say "no" politely – 80 different ways. (n.d.). Go Natural English. https://www.gonaturalenglish.com/how-to-say-no-politely/

How to speak no with ease in English. (2024, September 06). Learn Laugh Speak. https://learnlaughspeak.com/speak-no/

How to stop being a people pleaser (10 epic tips). (n.d.). Positive Thinking Mind. https://positivethinkingmind.com/stop-being-people-pleaser/

Humphrey, H. (n.d.). *How people-pleasing is affecting your career.* My Wellbeing. https://mywellbeing.com/workplace-wellbeing/people-pleasing-and-your-career

Kern, L. (2022, August 22). *Scripts for saying "no."* Leslie Kern Coaching. https://lesliekerncoaching.com/2022/08/22/scripts-for-saying-no/

Kim, J. (2023, July 18). *Break free from people-pleasing.* Psychology Today. https://www.psychologytoday.com/us/blog/the-angry-therapist/202307/break-free-from-people-pleasing

Kristenson, S. (2023, April 26). *11 smart goal examples to practice daily self-care.* Develop Good Habits. https://www.developgoodhabits.com/smart-goals-self-care/

Lamla, M. C. (2020, January 04). *Do narcissists actually lack empathy?* Psychology Today. https://www.psychologytoday.com/us/blog/intense-emotions-and-strong-feelings/202001/do-narcissists-actually-lack-empathy

Lawrence, H. (2023, May 07). *8 barriers to self-care that could impact your finances.* Clever Girl Finance. https://www.clevergirlfinance.com/.

Learning from setbacks: Turning challenges into opportunities. (2024, March 20). Inspire Mind Journey. https://inspiremindjourney.com/learning-from-setbacks/

Lerner, H. (2018, August 26). *10 relationship-saving tips for saying "no."* Psychology Today. https://www.psychologytoday.com/us/blog/the-dance-of-connection/201808/10-relationship-saving-tips-for-saying-no

Lo, I. (2021, March 25). *What it's like having a parent with borderline personality disorder*. Psychology Today. https://www.psychologytoday.com/gb/blog/living-with-emotional-intensity/202103/what-its-like-having-a-parent-with-borderline

Martin, S. (2021a, June 14). *4 strategies to cope with rejection*. Psychology Today. https://www.psychologytoday.com/us/blog/conquering-codependency/202106/4-strategies-to-cope-with-rejection

Martin, S. (2021b, January 04). *15 signs you're a people-pleaser*. Psychology Today. https://www.psychologytoday.com/us/blog/conquering-codependency/202101/15-signs-youre-a-people-pleaser

Martin, S. (2019, November 15). *Why it's so important to validate yourself and how to start*. PsychCentral. https://psychcentral.com/blog/imperfect/2019/11/why-its-so-important-to-validate-yourself-and-how-to-start

Martin, S. (2016, July 11). *How to deal with people who repeatedly violate your boundaries*. PsychCentral. https://psychcentral.com/blog/imperfect/2016/07/how-to-deal-with-people-who-repeatedly-violate-your-boundaries

Mayo Clinic Staff. (2023, November 30). *Job burnout: How to spot it and take action*. Mayo Clinic. https://www.mayoclinic.org/healthy-lifestyle/adult-health/in-depth/burnout/art-20046642

McCormack, M. (2023, March 20). *People-pleasing: Understanding the roots and consequences.* Counselling Directory. https://www.counselling-directory.org.uk/memberarticles/people-pleasing-understanding-the-roots-and-consequences

McLeod, S. (2024, February 02). *Operant conditioning: What it is, how it works, and examples.* Simply Psychology. https://www.simplypsychology.org/operant-conditioning.html

McQuald, M. (2024, September 30). *Avoid this common boundary-setting mistake.* Psychology Today. https://www.psychologytoday.com/us/blog/from-functioning-to-flourishing/202409/avoid-this-common-boundary-setting-mistake

Miller, K. (2020, March 13). *How to increase self-awareness: 16 activities & tools (+pdf).* PositivePsychology.com. https://positivepsychology.com/building-self-awareness-activities/

Moore, M. (2024, March 27). *The psychology behind people pleasing.* PsychCentral. https://psychcentral.com/health/the-need-to-please-the-psychology-of-people-pleasing

Nash, J. (2016, April 14). *How to accept the impermanence of life: A Buddhist take.* PositivePsychology.com. https://positivepsychology.com/impermanence/

Neff, K. (n.d.). *What is self-compassion?* Dr. Kristin Neff. https://self-compassion.org/what-is-self-compassion/

Nelson, M. (2023, May 06). *How people pleasing can affect relationships.* Psychology Today.

https://www.psychologytoday.com/us/blog/how-to-be-a-burden/202305/how-people-pleasing-can-affect-relationships

NeuroLaunch Editorial Team. (2024, September 22). *Aligning behavior and actions: The path to authentic living.* NeuroLaunch. https://neurolaunch.com/when-you-align-your-behavior-and-actions/

Newsonen, S. (2021, September 22). *7 strategies to make decisions with clarity and confidence.* Psychology Today. https://www.psychologytoday.com/us/blog/the-path-to-passionate-happiness/202109/7-strategies-to-make-decisions-with-clarity-and

Ni, P. (2015, October 11). *14 signs of psychological and emotional manipulation.* Psychology Today. https://www.psychologytoday.com/us/blog/communication-success/201510/14-signs-psychological-and-emotional-manipulation

Nickerson, C. (2023, October 16). *Symbolic interaction theory & examples.* Simply Psychology. https://www.simplypsychology.org/symbolic-interaction-theory.html

Nortje, A. (2021, February 27). *What is burnout? 16 signs and symptoms of excessive stress.* PositivePsychology.com. https://positivepsychology.com/burnout/

Onof, C. J. (n.d.). *Jean Paul Sartre: Existentialism.* Internet Encyclopedia of Philosophy. https://iep.utm.edu/Sartre-ex/

Operant conditioning. (2024, September 10). Wikipedia.
https://en.wikipedia.org/wiki/Operant_conditioning

Pederson, T. (2022, May 06). *How to be more self-aware and why it's important.* PsychCentral.
https://psychcentral.com/health/how-to-be-more-self-aware-and-why-its-important

People-pleasing. (n.d.). Psychology Today.
https://www.psychologytoday.com/intl/basics/people-pleasing#:~:text=More%20women%20than%20men%20do%20fall%20in%20this,would%20rather%20bend%20over%20backward%20than%20appear%20fussy.?msockid=294f886df6906a60268d9b69f7906bc7

Perfectionism. (2024, July 26). Mind Help.
https://mind.help/topic/perfectionism/

Perry, E. (2022, January 07). *How to say no to others (and why you shouldn't feel guilty).* BetterUp.
https://www.betterup.com/blog/how-to-say-no

Peters, B. (n.d.). *Five steps to identify your core values.* The Leadership Coaching Lab.
https://www.theleadershipcoachinglab.com/blog/identify-your-core-values

Pietrangelo, A. (2019, February 13). *What is fear of abandonment, and can it be treated?* Healthline.
https://www.healthline.com/health/fear-of-abandonment

Plattor, C. (n.d.). *Codependency and recovery: The truth about people-pleasing.* Codependency Recovery.
https://codependencyrecovery.org/2022/10/03/codep

endency-and-recovery-the-truth-about-people-
pleasing/

Porter, D. (2024, May 02). *10 ways people pleasing can affect
your relationship.* Marriage.com.
https://www.marriage.com/advice/relationship/how-
people-pleasing-can-affect-
relationships/#How_people_pleasing_can_affect_rela
tionships_10_things_to_consider

Pradeepa, S. (2023, November 14). *Characteristics of
trustworthiness: 15 top qualities.* Believe In Mind.
https://www.believeinmind.com/personality/character
istics-of-trustworthiness/

Precker, M. (2022, October 12). *How job burnout can hurt
your health – and what to do about it.* American Heart
Association.
https://www.heart.org/en/news/2022/10/12/how-job-
burnout-can-hurt-your-health-and-what-to-do-about-it

Prosser, S., Rehn, A., & Born, N. (n.d.). *How can you use pitch
variation to make your message engaging?* LinkedIn.
https://www.linkedin.com/advice/0/how-can-you-
use-pitch-variation-make-your-message-
6y0yf#:~:text=A%20higher%20pitch%20can%20be%2
0used%20to%20express,main%20argument%20or%2
0presenting%20a%20fact%20or%20statistic.

Quinlan, C. (2024, May 02). *7 ways to handle a partner who
is disrespecting boundaries.* Marriage.com.
https://www.marriage.com/advice/relationship/disres
pecting-your-boundaries/

Quoteresearch. (2016, August 28). *It is not the mountain we conquer, but ourselves.* Quote Investigator. https://quoteinvestigator.com/2016/08/18/conquer/

Ratson, M. (2023, December 18). *How to defend your boundaries and be assertive.* Psychology Today. https://www.psychologytoday.com/us/blog/the-wisdom-of-anger/202312/how-to-defend-your-boundaries-and-be-assertive

Ratson, M. (2022, February 14). *How to determine if someone is trustworthy.* WikiHow. https://www.wikihow.com/Determine-if-Someone-Is-Trustworthy

Salvagioni, D. A. J., Melanda, F. N., Mesas, A. E., González, A. D., Gabani, F. L., & Andrade, S. M. D. (2017). Physical, psychological and occupational consequences of job burnout: A systematic review of prospective studies. *Public Library of Science One, 12*(10), e0185781.

Scott, E. (2023, February 23). *The importance of setting boundaries for mental health.* Verywell Mind. https://www.verywellmind.com/setting-boundaries-for-stress-management-3144985

Scott, E. (2024, June 12). *How to recognize burnout symptoms.* Verywell Mind. https://www.verywellmind.com/stress-and-burnout-symptoms-and-causes-3144516#toc-symptoms-you-might-be-experiencing-burnout

Scott, S. J. (2023, April 24). *13 steps to celebrate small wins with your goals.* Develop Good Habits. https://www.developgoodhabits.com/power-of-small-wins/

Scott, S. J. (2022, October 14). *5 steps to write your personal mission statement (with examples)*. Develop Good Habits. https://www.developgoodhabits.com/personal-mission-statement/

Shapiro, J. (2021, February 26). *Balancing the needs of self and others*. Psychology Today. https://www.psychologytoday.com/us/blog/thinking-in-black-white-and-gray/202102/balancing-the-needs-self-and-others

Short-term financial stability: A foundation for security and well-being. (2019, April 24). The Aspen Institute. https://www.aspeninstitute.org/publications/short-term-financial-stability-a-foundation-for-security-and-well-being/

Signs you're a people-pleaser — and how to stop. (2023, September 26). Cleveland Clinic. https://health.clevelandclinic.org/how-to-stop-being-a-people-pleaser

Sinn, M. P. (2020, December 05). *Subconscious processes 27,500 times more data than the conscious mind.* Think by Numbers. https://thinkbynumbers.org/psychology/subconscious-processes-27500-times-more-data-than-the-conscious-mind/

Smith, M. (2023, May 21). *People-pleasers are at a higher risk of burnout, says Harvard-trained psychologist—how to spot the signs.* CNBC. https://www.cnbc.com/2023/05/21/harvard-trained-psychologist-people-pleasers-are-at-higher-risk-for-burnout.html

Sockolov, E. (2024, September 03). *5 ways to validate yourself, and why it's important.* One Mind Therapy. https://onemindtherapy.com/therapy/how-to-validate-yourself/

Streed, J. (2024, September 28). *Mayo Clinic q and a: Setting boundaries for your well-being.* Mayo Clinic News Network. https://newsnetwork.mayoclinic.org/discussion/mayo-clinic-q-and-a-setting-boundaries-for-your-well-being/

Swamy, C. (2022, May 27). *How to recover from people pleasing.* Ama La Vida. https://alvcoaching.com/blog/how-to-recover-from-people-pleasing/

Sweeney, K. (2023, October 26). *40 ways to pamper yourself because you're worth it.* Byrde. https://www.byrdie.com/how-to-pamper-yourself-5112735

Swider, B., Harari, D., Breidenthal, A. P., & Steed, L. B. (2018). *The pros and cons of perfectionism, according to research.* Harvard Business Review. https://hbr.org/2018/12/the-pros-and-cons-of-perfectionism-according-to-research

Tanasugarn, A. (2022a, August 13). *How people-pleasing damages self-worth.* Psychology Today. https://www.psychologytoday.com/us/blog/understanding-ptsd/202208/how-people-pleasing-damages-self-worth

Tanasugarn, A. (2022b, December 26). *The long-term effect of being raised by a borderline parent.* Psychology Today. https://www.psychologytoday.com/us/blog/understan

ding-ptsd/202212/the-legacy-of-being-raised-by-a-borderline-parent

Tartakovsky, M. (2015, August 07). *10 simple questions to help you identify or clarify your needs*. PsychCentral. https://psychcentral.com/blog/weightless/2015/08/10-simple-questions-to-help-you-identify-or-clarify-your-needs#1

Tassinari, M. (2022, October 31). *5 common boundary myths debunked and truths revealed*. Martha Tassinari. https://www.marthatassinari.com/blog/5-common-boundary-myths-debunked-and-truths-revealed

Telloian, C. (2021, November 10). *The tactic narcissistic personalities often use on empathic people*. PsychCentral. https://psychcentral.com/disorders/narcissistic-projection

Teuber, M., Leyhr, D., & Sudeck, G. (2024). Physical activity improves stress load, recovery, and academic performance-related parameters among university students: A longitudinal study on daily level. *BMC Public Health, 24*(1), 598. https://doi.org/10.1186/s12889-024-18082-z

The psychology of people-pleasing: Causes and strategies for overcoming approval-seeking behavior. (2024, March 06). Resilient Roots Psychotherapy. https://www.resilientrootspsychotherapy.com/blog/overcoming-people-pleasing

Therapist.com Team. (2024, August 13). *Burnout: Stages, types, causes, and signs*. Therapist.com. https://therapist.com/stress/burnout/

The science of celebrating: How joyous occasions benefit your health. (n.d.). The Wellness Engineer. https://www.thewellnessengineer.com/blog/the-science-of-celebrating-how-joyous-occasions-benefit-your-health

Thomas, B. (2024, October 04). *The 5 means of communication: Exploring the different channels for effective interaction.* GCELT. https://gcelt.org/the-5-means-of-communication-exploring-the-different-channels-for-effective-interaction/

Tulgan, B. (2020, October 13). *Overcommitment syndrome leads to siege mentality at work.* Psychology Today. https://www.psychologytoday.com/us/blog/navigating-the-new-workplace/202010/overcommitment-syndrome-leads-to-siege-mentality-at-work

20 smart examples: How to say "no" politely. (n.d.). Status.net. https://status.net/articles/say-no-politely-smart-examples/

Umlas, R. (2024, June 23). *How to tell if someone is trustworthy: 10 key indicators.* Hack Spirit. https://hackspirit.com/how-to-tell-if-someone-is-trustworthy/

Understanding people pleasers. (2023, April 30). The Psychology Practice. https://thepsychpractice.com/plog/2023/4/30/understanding-people-pleasers#google_vignette

Understanding selfishness vs. self-care. (2020, October 27). First Step Recovery & Travco Behavioral Health. https://www.wecaremoreohio.com/blog/understanding-selfishness-vs-self-care

Unlocking your desires: A guide to figuring out what you want in life. (2023, July 06). Tru and Well. https://truandwell.com/health-and-wellness/figuring-out-what-you-want-in-life/

Van Edwards, V. (2024a, June 04). *11 expert tips to stop being a people pleaser and start doing you.* Science of People. https://www.scienceofpeople.com/people-pleaser/#1-%e2%80%9clet-me-get-back-to-you%e2%80%9d

Van Edwards, V. (2024b, June 04). *6 effective tips to politely say no (that actually work!).* Science of People. https://www.scienceofpeople.com/how-to-say-no/

Vermani, M. (2023, December 12). *Breaking bad: People pleasing.* Psychology Today. https://www.psychologytoday.com/intl/blog/a-deeper-wellness/202312/breaking-bad-people-pleasing

Vigliotti, A. (2023, October 24). *Why people-pleasing isn't pleasing anyone.* Psychology Today. https://www.psychologytoday.com/us/blog/the-now/202310/why-people-pleasing-isnt-pleasing-anyone

Villines, Z. (2023, November 30). *What to know about abandonment issues.* Medical News Today. https://www.medicalnewstoday.com/articles/325792#summary

Vinney, C. (2024, June 07). *What is self-concept in psychology?* ThoughtCo. https://www.thoughtco.com/self-concept-psychology-4176368

Vogel, K. (2023, February 07). *Pay it forward! Here are 97 ways to show appreciation to those you care about.* Parade. https://parade.com/1208701/kaitlin-vogel/how-to-show-appreciation/#:~:text=Show%20up%20on%20time,%20keep%20promises%20and%20do%20what

Volume. (n.d.). Fiveable. https://library.fiveable.me/key-terms/leadership-communication/volume

Watson, S. (2024, April 18). *Endorphins: The brain's natural pain reliever.* Harvard Health. https://www.health.harvard.edu/mind-and-mood/endorphins-the-brains-natural-pain-reliever

Well.org. (2019, March 12). *How your subconscious mind controls your behavior.* Well.org Blog. https://well.org/mindset/how-your-subconscious-mind-controls-your-behavior/

Wilding, M. (2022, March 10). *How to stop overthinking and start trusting your gut.* Harvard Business Review. https://hbr.org/2022/03/how-to-stop-overthinking-and-start-trusting-your-gut

Wright, P. (2022, September 18). *Your brain on laughter: What happens in your brain when you laugh?* Nuvance Health. https://www.nuvancehealth.org/health-tips-and-news/your-brain-on-laughter

Yoon, Y. (2023, December 04). *Navigating relationships: The power of healthy boundaries.* Psychology Today. https://www.psychologytoday.com/us/blog/on-second-thought/202311/navigating-relationships-the-power-of-healthy-boundaries

Image References

Altmann, G. (2018, October 22). *Social media TikTok connection* [image]. Pixabay. https://pixabay.com/illustrations/social-media-connection-concept-3758364/

Chan, A. (2017, June 03). *This Is the sign you've been looking for neon signage* [image]. Unsplash. https://unsplash.com/photos/this-is-the-sign-youve-been-looking-for-neon-signage-ukzHlkoz1IE

Duckleap. (2023, December 11). Woman, self-love, love [image]. Pixabay. https://pixabay.com/illustrations/woman-self-love-love-hug-8439000/

Ferreira, D. (2020, April 15). *Black and brown train rail* [image]. Unsplash. https://unsplash.com/photos/black-and-brown-train-rail-ZaowsoETAu0

Hagan, J. (2022, May 26). *An open book sitting on top of a bed next to a pencil* [image]. Unsplash. https://unsplash.com/photos/an-open-book-sitting-on-top-of-a-bed-next-to-a-pencil-0Wx3kEFdgjQ

Henry, M. (n.d.). *Wooden judge gravel* [image]. Shopify. https://www.shopify.com/stock-photos/photos/wooden-judge-gavel?q=truth

Hoahoa111. (2021, February 03). *Cafe, girl, book* [image]. Pixabay. https://pixabay.com/photos/cafe-girl-book-reading-read-drink-5972490/

Kaboompics, K. (2020, October 28). *Close-up shot of a woman holding a credit card and smartphone* [image]. Pexels. https://www.pexels.com/photo/close-up-shot-of-a-woman-holding-a-credit-card-and-smartphone-5717934/

Kukanauskas, V. (2023, November 20). *AI generated work, business, exhausted royalty-free stock illustration* [image]. Pixabay. https://pixabay.com/illustrations/work-business-exhausted-burnout-8396641/

Lark, B. (2017, January 21). *Woman holding white mug while standing* [image]. Unsplash. https://unsplash.com/photos/woman-holding-white-mug-while-standing-nMffL1zjbw4

Mart Production. (2021, May 03). *Woman in white tank top holding plastic* [image]. Pexels. https://www.pexels.com/photo/woman-in-white-tank-top-holding-plastic-7767766/

Naranjo, B. (2014, July 21). *Silhouette of a couple sitting on boat during sunset* [image]. Pixabay. https://pixabay.com/illustrations/digital-art-couple-silhouettes-398342/

Nik. (2018, June 11). *Difficult roads lead to beautiful destinations quote on desk decor* [image]. Unsplash. https://unsplash.com/photos/difficult-roads-lead-to-beautiful-destinations-desk-decor-z1d-LP8sjuI

Nilov, M. (2021, August 17). *A close-up shot of golf cart pedals* [image]. Pexels. https://www.pexels.com/photo/a-close-up-shot-of-golf-cart-pedals-9207748/

Pexels. (2016, November 21). *King, chess, checkmate board* [image]. Pixabay. https://pixabay.com/photos/king-chess-checkmate-board-game-1846807/

Shopify Photos. (n.d.). *Celebration sparkler and decor* [image]. Shopify. https://www.shopify.com/stock-photos/photos/celebration-sparkler-and-decor?q=Celebrate+Your+Progress+and+Victories

Shuraeva, A. (2021, September 09). *Team doing hands together* [image]. Pexels. https://www.pexels.com/photo/team-doing-hands-together-9501978/

SHVETS Production. (2021, March 17). *Crop unrecognizable female psychologist and patient discussing mental problems during session* [image]. Pexels. https://www.pexels.com/photo/crop-unrecognizable-female-psychologist-and-patient-discussing-mental-problems-during-session-7176319/

Ziegler, R. (2023, August 24). *Self-love, self-consciousness, self-confidence* [image]. Pixabay. https://pixabay.com/illustrations/self-love-self-consciousness-8207755/

Ziegler, R. (2022, July 09). *Woman, flower, grow* [image]. Pixabay. https://pixabay.com/illustrations/woman-flower-grow-self-love-7306978/

72594201R00105